The Christian Woman
. . . Set Free

Library of Congress Cataloging-in-Publication Data

Edwards, Gene
  The Christian Woman...Set Free / Gene Edwards
  ISBN 0-9778033-0-9
  1. Bible Non-Fiction. I. Title.

SeedSowers Publishing
P.O. Box 3317
Jacksonville, FL 32206
800-228-2665
www.seedsowers.com

Books by Gene Edwards

DEDICATION

This book is dedicated to men not yet born, men who will one day be men called of God. It falls to you, also, to take up the task of ensuring the equality of Christian women in the churches of your generation. As long as translators continue to mistranslate the same old bias into verses in I Corinthians Eleven and Fourteen, Ephesians Five and I Timothy Two, then there will be those who teach that women should wear head covering, and not speak in meetings, and generally imply that women are inferior to men in the kingdom of God. It will therefore fall to those of you in future generations to continue the task of setting women free to equality in the church.

ACKNOWLEDGMENTS

To my daughter Lynda who—knowing of my interest in history, urged me to study the history of women. This book would not have existed if I had not followed her request . . . not to mention it changed my life forever regarding womanhood.

To Helen, my wife, the best editor whose steady hand can be found in all my books.

To Kathy McGraw, my associate, without whom there would be no books.

To my secretary Deanna Snell who has mastered the art of reading my handwriting.

THE
AUTHOR'S CONFESSION

It is ironic that I, of all people, would be writing a book about women. I grew up among some of the toughest men in the world. That is, I grew up in the midst of the Texas oil fields surrounded by workers known as "rough necks." Further, I am one of five boys. Because of my parents' divorce, I grew up not only in a world with hardly any women in sight, but I continued in this rough and rugged world until my heart was smitten by the lady who became my wife.

I am told that churches have a ratio of two women for every man in Sunday morning church services. That was never true in my experience as a young pastor. Men always outnumbered women. The reason was that instead of just sitting in pews, the men in the church functioned.

Later, when I began pioneering in *the house church movement*, the men in these churches quite literally led the church. (These particular house churches are all lay-led. There are no resident pastors in any of these churches.)

Later I realized, rather slowly, that women could also lead just as well as did men. (Ladies, I confess a time lag between those two points and offer no defense for this oversight.)

So, it was at that time we began making discoveries previously unknown concerning joint participation and joint leadership in the churches. In this adventure we literally "marched off the map" into an unexplored world of which we, men or women, had never dreamed.

The greatest surprise in all this was the reaction of the men as they found themselves part of a church where the women were co-functioning with the men. This reaction was one of both surprise and joy. Styles and approaches are *different* among the two genders, but the variety and creativity which resulted was far beyond anything we had anticipated.

"Laymen" have always been surprised to learn that they can be the entire leadership of the church; but even more, all are surprised that the women are good at this, too.

You will find this book constantly brings to you a whole new "wrinkle" on the evangelical mind. With the issue of *The Christian Women . . . Set Free,* it is our intention to see more saints finding the sheer glory of this unique journey into freedom.

Please join me in a world where churches are led by men and women together under the headship of Christ. And wonder with me, why the New Testament story, so evident in its esteemed presentation of women, has been so long overlooked. There is no higher calling than to be co-pioneers of rediscovering forgotten paths.

(And yes, in most of the house churches the men still outnumber the women.)

Contents

CONTENTS

PART VII
Making This Practical

ADDENDA

You are not going to like the
following quotes . . . neither do I.
                                    —G.E.

Praise be to God that he has not created
me a Gentile, a woman, or a hog.
                    —Hebrew Prayer

The courage of a man is shown in his ability to command. The courage of a woman is found in obeying.

—Aristotle

By all means get married. If you get
a good wife, you will be happy. If
you get a bad wife, you will become
a philosopher.

—Socrates

Women are those who fell prey to their irrational, emotional side, and are therefore incapable of reason and making rational choices . . . moreover as irrational beings, women may not always know what they really want, and so it is the man's domain to decide for them.

—Plato

We have courtesans for our sex and pleasure. We have young slave prostitutes for our physical use and we have wives to bring up legitimate children.

—Demosthenes

Do not admire your wife's beauty . . . from the time women are fourteen years old they think of nothing and aim at nothing except going to bed with men.

—Epictetus

Even the most virtuous of women is a witch.

—Oral Jewish Law

Woman is a temple built over a sewer. It is contrary to the order of nature and of the law for women to speak in a gathering.

—Saint Jerome

Because of you we are punished by death
. . . because of you, women, the Son of
God had to die.

—Tertullian

Men should not listen to a woman even if she says admirable things or if she says saintly things. They are of little consequence since they come from the mouth of a woman.

—Origen

A man may marry again if he has divorced his sinful wife because he is not restricted in his right as is the woman, because he is her head.

—Ambrose

By herself woman is not of the image of
God. The man, on the other hand, alone,
is the image of God

—Augustine

For a man to go to a woman for advice is like going to the lowest kind of animal to seek advice.

—Chrysostom

Woman is defective and misbegotten.

—Aquinas

The wickedness of women is greater than all other wickedness. A dragon is more curable than the familiarity of a woman. Avoid them like poisonous animals.

—Pope Innocence III

There is no gown or garment that worse becomes a woman than when she would be wise.

—Martin Luther

All women are born that they may acknowledge themselves as inferior to the male.

—Calvin

To make women learned and to make a fox tame work out to the same end. Educating a woman or a fox simply makes them more cunning.

—King James

The quotes which you have just read may cause a reaction in you; nevertheless, these words did not move me to write this book. But the quote on the next page did! In fact, having heard the next statement, I went home and started this book!

—Gene Edwards

You would not let an eleven-year-old child stand up in a meeting and talk. Then why should you allow a woman to speak in a meeting?

—A statement made in a Christian conference in the twenty-first century

PART I

Who Started the Mistreatment of Women?

One

A Time Past Due

This is not so much a book as it is a declaration of war.

You are about to be introduced to over two thousand years of abuse of womanhood throughout the Western world. You are also about to see seventeen hundred years of the subjugation of Christian womanhood throughout church history. This book you hold in your hand exists for the purpose of lifting women from that second-class citizenship.

Some of the historical facts in this book will shock you. By the time you read the last chapter, I trust you will be free from perceiving any sense of second-class citizenship as coming from the Scriptures or from the early church.

If you happen to be a fellow male, it is my prayer that you will rise to take your place in seeing an end to this stigma which places women in a position inferior to men.

Jesus Christ does not discriminate against women. In all the annals of human history, He was the greatest of all women liberators, even breathtakingly so.

Then there is Paul.

To some, he is a male chauvinist and maybe even a woman hater. But you will discover that Paul, like his Lord, was also a liberator of women.

If this be true, and it is, then there must be some serious mistranslation of I Corinthians Eleven and Fourteen, as well as Ephesians Five, and I Timothy Two. Stand in horror that these mistranslations have been carried from century to century, beginning in A. D. 405, until this very day.

A final word about this book.

There are men who tell women they must wear doilies on their heads and never speak in the church. Sirs, when you finish this book you will either renounce these views or stand in embarrassment to discover you are keeping company with some of the worst voices of men who ever spoke ill of women throughout all the annals of Western civilization.

Now, take my hand. We will travel to the land where man's *very* low view of women began.

Come with me to a grove of trees in Athens, Greece.

Two

It All Began With Philosophers

The Greek view of women has molded man's attitude toward women.

The Greek view of the world influenced Europe; but later, after the Greeks conquered the Middle East (300 B.C.), they greatly influenced thought in Israel. The Greeks not only influenced the Jewish mind but, unfortunately, later the Christian mind.

Three men, all who taught in Athens, fathered the Western mind. All three men had a shockingly low view of women.

(Ironically, Athens was named after a woman.)

These men are Socrates, his student Plato, and Plato's student Aristotle. Aristotle in turn taught Alexander the Great, who, in turn, spread the Greek mind to the world.

Socrates believed that the creation of women was a result of divine punishment. He declared that women should have all the *duties* of a man, but none of the *privileges*. One of his rhetorical questions was, "In all the species, is it not obvious that the male is far superior to the female?" He also asked, "Is there anyone to whom you talk less than to your wife?" And "By all means get married. If you get a good wife, you will be happy. If you get a bad wife, you will become a philosopher."

Socrates' disciple would become more influential than he himself was. (Plato 470 to 347 B.C.)

Plato's disciple (Aristotle 384 to 322 B.C.) is often seen as a hero in the Western world. Alas, our hero was actually paid to philosophize that slavery was a necessary institution of society.

Aristotle supposedly gave us *scientific* observation and the science of logical thought. He failed at both, and as a result he is called the father of the Dark Ages. His approach to logical observation, adopted by the world, brought to an early end the empirical method of science. As a result, he set us back at least one thousand years in the world of science. Aristotle's conclusions about women were just as dark or even darker.

Behold the logician: Aristotle noticed that a bee would lead the entire beehive *into a swarm*. In Aristotle's mind, since man was so much more adapted to leadership than women were, he announced that this bee in leadership was the king bee. (Hence, "*Aristotelian logic.*") The bee turned out to be a *queen*.

Aristotle continued his logic by declaring that there was inequality between man and woman, and therefore men should not distinguish between a *wife* and a *slave*. In Aristotle's exact words,

> The courage of a man is shown in his ability
> to command. The courage of a woman is
> found in obeying.

Then there was a contemporary of Aristotle, Demosthenes, known to be the greatest orator that Greece ever produced.

> We have courtesans* for our sex and pleasure. We have young slave prostitutes for our physical use, and we have wives to bring up legitimate children.

And there was Pericles, who was Athens' leading citizen.

> An Athenian mother should live a life so retired that her name would never be mentioned among men. She would neither be shamed nor praised.

Then there was Zeno, a disciple of Socrates (circa 400 B.C.). Zeno was a thinker and a man who had great influence on the Greek mind and the Roman mind.

Zeno objected to the way men used women, that is, only for pleasure. His reason? Pleasure kept men from studying philosophy! Zeno taught that men should only have sex to produce children. This idea found its way into Roman Catholicism. (He also taught that celibacy is to be preferred over marriage, also later found in Catholic thought.)

Zeno is, in fact, one of the great influences on fourth-century Christianity. Christian history records that Plato, Aristotle, and Zeno were embraced by Christianity. Zeno's *asceticism* gave rise to the era of the monks. He is the co-founder of The Desert Fathers, who attempted to get away from the world—especially the central evil of the world,

---

* These were upper class prostitutes. In Greek they were called *hetairai.*

women. A man who was married could not reach spiritual maturity, which is still a shadowy part of Catholic theology. Why cannot a married man be a priest? Because he cannot become spiritual.

And now you know!

But let us look upon one more Greek thinker who downed women.

Epictetus (A.D. 90) did not believe there was anything good to be said about women. To wit:

> Do not admire your wife's beauty. . . . From the time women are fourteen years old they think of nothing and aim at nothing except going to bed with men.

(Any chance he was blaming women for his own problem?)

In Epictetus' mind, women were nothing but a temptation to men. Now, meet the prevailing sentiment of that day: "They lure men with soft voices."

So, we must ask, what then was life like for a woman living in Athens?

Women led a life of seclusion. They took no part in government. (Keep all this in mind when Paul wrote to the *Greeks* living in Corinth, a city just south of Athens.) For a woman to speak in an assembly in Greece would be unlawful and a terrible embarrassment to her husband. Women never appeared at social functions or outdoor sports. The Agora (the marketplace) was a man's domain. Women were not allowed there.

Instead, women were to "see as little as possible, hear as little as possible, ask as little as possible." Men spoke very few words to women.

Women were usually married to men they had never met prior to their marriage. Generally speaking, women received no education except in how to cook and perform other household duties. Women were taught to be quiet. The women of Athens never went out alone. They never shared meals with men.

They had no part in government or community affairs. They lived in seclusion. With few exceptions, they were illiterate.

One Athenian describes his marriage in this way, "My wife was not yet fifteen when I introduced her to my household. She had been brought up under the strictest supervision. She has not been allowed to see anything, hear anything, or to ask any questions."

(At this point, please begin to wonder what happened when the Gospel reached Greece.)

In Summary

You have been affected by all of this attitude. The Greeks gave us our Western mind. What then, was life for a woman in day-to-day living?

Classic Greek philosophers taught that women were a distraction from all aspects of life and "half-way between a human and an animal."

It can all be said in one sentence:

> Women should not see anything, should   not
> hear anything, and should not ask anything.

Such was the life of women in the Greek world.

Enter the Christian era.

Did life for women get better, or did the Greek view of womankind get into Christianity? It is important for all of us to know the answer.

PART II

The Church's Subjugation of Women from A.D. 100 until . . .

Let us look at the world's *most* influential men:

      a monk called Jerome

      the early fathers

      men of the *very* Dark Ages

      the Reformers

      a king named James

Three

Century Two to Constantine
(A.D. 100-400)

Did the Greek views of women change at the time of the Christian faith, or did the Greek views of women influence the Christian faith?

Enter Jerome. Jerome is one of the most influential Christians of all time and, for some, a candidate for being the most hated man in Christian history. This man was just possibly not only the single most influential man in all the post-apostolic era, he is probably the most influential man in influencing the views of women. He was a woman hater of the first order.

He also authored the most influential translation of the New Testament in all history. He is the man who went out of his way to translate I Corinthians Eleven and Fourteen, I Timothy Two and Ephesians Five in such a way as to put women in the worst possible light.

Jerome was the worst woman hater in all the long history of Christianity.

No less a scholar and historian than Will Durant (the dean of history) wrote, "Jerome had a morbid prurience (lewdness) . . . a man not free from the heat of desire. Some of the writings of Jerome border on madness."

I agree. Jerome was mean. When someone disagreed with him, he would vehemently enter into an almost uncontrollable rage. He ranted and raved throughout his entire adult life.

What he ranted against most was sexual immorality. Sex was Jerome's central topic. In fact, he was obsessed with it. (Out of the mouth the heart speaks.) Some of his writings about sex and women are so vivid that one is quite reluctant to quote the man.

In one of Jerome's letters, he scolds a woman for her *perceived* worldliness. One dare not place the letter in a book. It is incredibly vivid in its description. That is, describing what he *thought* she was thinking! *

Let me hasten to say that Jerome has been sainted by the Roman Catholic Church and is one of Catholic history's most revered men. Jerome and another influential man named Augustine were contemporaries. Both have been honored with the title *Doctor of the Church*. Jerome's views of women are embedded in the teachings of Augustine.

Again a strong case could be made that Jerome is the greatest single influence in Christian history. Regarding women, and sex, Jerome is the single most influential person in Christian history, and his views reign even to this hour.

How can that be true even today in so enlightened an age? Because he gave the world the most influential translation of the New Testament ever, and his mistranslations about women still remain in virtually every subsequent translation. Even today, he still influences the words we speak and has shaped the thinking of all believers.

---

*Throughout his life, Jerome never stopped railing against women. He believed in an ascetic life. He believed this was the one way to not think about sex, although he did write about what he did not think about. Even his bishop counseled him about his obsession with sex. He turned on his bishop and attacked him, calling his bishop ignorant, brutish, wicked, well-matched to the worldly flock, and the unskillful pilot of a crazy bark (ship). When someone is obsessed with sin as much as he was, it betrays, at least, a sick mind.

Have you ever noticed the words in italics in your New Testament? Those italicized words mean that *those* words are not in the original text, but were added to clarify *or* interpret the sentence. Have you ever wondered *who* started this practice and who chose what to interpret and emphasize?

Answer: Jerome. Jerome also did something else which affects you every time you read the Bible!* Jerome declared that only monks could be true Christians. (A monk is free from property, lust, and pride.)

And what did he say about women?

> Woman is a temple built over a sewer.
> It is contrary to the order of nature and of the law for women to speak in a gathering. Women, especially those who assume leadership roles in religion, are miserable, sin-ridden wretches.

Jerome opposed women's speaking, singing, praying, or teaching in public.

"If you cannot live in a convent, then live a life of a virgin."

(Jerome gave that advice to married women! He came very close to calling marriage a sin.)

"I praise marriage only this far: marriage produces virgins for me." He felt strongly that the only way anyone could be a decent Christian was to be a virgin!

Another of his famous statements was, "Cut down the wood of marriage by the axe of virginity!"

---

*If you would like to read more about this man, (more than I dare print), then you might want to look in the book entitled *The Age of Faith,* by Will Durant, pages 51 to 55, for a small glance at this man's vast influence.

And, "Virginity can be lost even by thought!"

(By the way, Jerome believed in sinless perfection!)

Now you have some idea of where some Christian leaders of our day have acquired some of their views of women.

In the fifth century, the Roman Catholic church announced Jerome's translation to be the only inspired translation of the Bible, now and forever world without end.

It got worse.

Later, anyone caught reading a Bible other than the Jerome translation would be killed that very day.

Will Durant may have said it best. "Jerome was a saint only in the sense that he lived an ascetic life. He was a great man, but he was not a good man."

Keep in mind, all the leaders of the Reformation were reading Jerome's New Testament. And that, dear reader, is how Jerome's misinterpretations still affect womankind today.

Thomas Aquinas, Martin Luther and John Calvin all adopted his translation, which was not kind to women. Nor were any of these men kind to women.

Here is a little-known and ironic fact: Jerome acknowledged that two women helped him translate his Bible! When the church fathers later found this out, they erased the names of the two women and wrote the words "venerable brothers."

Ladies take note!

Jerome was worth a chapter.

Yes, and things get worse.

There were others in this period (A.D. 100-400) who had much to say about women.

Let us now hear from these Greek-philosophers-turned-Christian; that is, read what the venerable church fathers had to say about women!

Four

The Early Church Fathers

Historians call the Christians who wrote theological documents in the early years of the Christian faith "the early church fathers." But that is a misnomer. These "fathers" are merely men whose writings survived. We will never know the ways of Christians in the local body of believers in the third century. Why? Because only philosophers have a predisposition to write! Their philosophy does not tell us what that period was really like in the simple gatherings of the ekklesia.

Most of the men you are about to meet were pagan philosophers before they turned Christian. Unfortunately, they blended many of their pagan views into their Christian faith. And that pagan part is reflected in Greek views of women.

> There is nothing for a man that is shameful, for man is endowed with reason. But for women, it brings shame to even reflect on what she is.
> —Clement of Alexander (A.D. 150-220)

Clement also taught that women should be veiled. Reason? So that men would not be tempted to sin!

Then there is Tertullian (A.D. 160-240) who is one of the fathers of the Latin church. He is usually greatly respected among church historians, but he has also been called the first Christian misogynist.* Tertullian called women "the Devil's gateway." And,

"Because of you we are punished by death . . . because of you (women) the Son of God had to die."

Tertullian used I Corinthians Fourteen to silence women. He declared that they should neither baptize, sing, pray, nor teach. Then there was the unmarried philosopher named Origen (A.D. 185-250). He was one of the most interesting of the early church fathers. After the death of his father, Origen took over his father's theology classes, at age seventeen. Upon taking that position, he had himself castrated so he would not be bothered by women! But that did not keep him from having some strong opinions about them.

Men should not listen to a woman even if she says admirable things or if she says saintly things. That is of little consequence since they come from the mouth of a woman.

So, you see, these anti-women views were so embedded that even a surgical operation did not help! Origen also said:

What is seen with the eyes of the Creator is masculine *and not* feminine, for God does not stoop to look upon what is feminine.

---

*One who hates women.

20

We come now to the much-venerated Ambrose of Milan (A.D. 340-397). (He led Augustine to the Lord.) Ambrose believed that Eve was seductive and, as a result of that seduction, was the root of all evil and of all lies.

> Even though man was created outside of paradise, he is found to be superior, while woman, though created in a better place, is found inferior.

Ambrose wrote:

> She who does not have faith is a woman and should be called by the name of her sex. But she who believes progresses to perfect manhood. When this happens she does away with the name of her sex. . . . A man may marry again if he has divorced his sinful wife because he is not restricted in his right as is the woman, because he is her head.

We now ascend to the great theologian Augustine (A.D. 354-430). He is the most popular and best known of the church fathers. Augustine lived in North Africa. He died just as the Roman Empire was collapsing. Augustine's theology laid the foundation of orthodox theology in the West. Prior to becoming a Christian, Augustine was an open and admitted womanizer. Then, as a Christian, he held women in low esteem. He taught that only Adam was made in the image of God. He has been called the ultimate misogynist.

By herself woman is not of the image of God.
The man, on the other hand, alone, is the image
of God. . . . We should look upon the female
state as if it were being a deformity.

Augustine believed that women were inherently evil. He
blamed woman exclusively for the Fall:

Eve was the first to be deceived and was responsible for deceiving man. She made her husband a
partaker of the evil of which she herself was con-
scious.

Augustine was not satisfied with blaming woman for the
Fall. He also blamed women for the *Flood*!

Cyril of Alexandria (circa A.D. 400) went far beyond hating
women. He believed that women were inferior and could not
teach men; but, alas, Cyril was more than a philosopher, he was
a pragmatic. He put philosophy into action. There was a very
brilliant woman in Alexandria named Hypatia who proved Cyril
wrong on the subjects of mathematics and philosophy. She went
so far as to speak out against his teachings (A.D. 415). The
monks who followed Cyril murdered Hypatia inside a church
building! They burned her flesh as they tore it from her bones!

We now come to Chrysostom (A.D. 347-407), another
"church father." John Chrysostom is a man who is not difficult
to dislike. At one time he was the lead clergyman in the city of
Constantinople. He is considered the greatest orator of the East-
ern church. He later became the leading clergyman in the city of
Antioch, Syria. (Thanks go to Chrysostom for the Sunday morning sermon.)

His view of women?

"Eve taught once and ruined all."

Chrysostom believed that woman did not possess the image of God and confined her to a subordinate state. Woman was inferior to man.

> (Her low estate) was not simply a result of the Fall. Woman was an inferior person even at the moment of her creation. . . . Image has to do with authority, and only man has that . . . . Man is subjective to no one while woman is subjective to man. . . . For a man to go to a woman for advice is like going to an animal of the lowest kind to seek advice.

There you have it, the pagan view of the leaders of Christianity in its formative years. When the first Christian century ended, the view and the place of Christian women was high and equitable, but after the Greek view of women slipped into the Christian faith from these pagan-philosophers-turned-Christian, their view predominated.

You who work hard at making women second-class citizens in the kingdom of God, please note the company you keep!

Next comes the view of women during the Dark Ages. They called it *dark* for a very good reason. If you thought the situation was bad, wait until you see the world from A.D. 506 to 1100.

The following chapter is rated *X* for *excruciating!*

Five

The Darkness
of the Dark Ages

Witches. Hangings. Burnings.

Celibacy, man's escape from the wiles of women, came into full bloom in this age of the *demonizing* of women.

The fiery stake was in much use in those days.

(At this point you might want to guess how many women were burned at the stake for being witches. Later we will find the answer.)

We come to Thomas Aquinas (died in 1247). He was a monk. He was also the Catholic church's premier theologian.

(Monks had a very dim view of women. After all, it was the woman who made man lust.)

His Catholic view of women later came over into Protestant theology.

Aquinas taught that women are spiritually, biologically, and intellectually inferior to men.

> Woman is defective and misbegotten. . . . Woman
> is naturally subject to man because in man the
> discernment of wisdom predominates.

Aquinas stated that woman did not have sufficient wisdom of herself; therefore, she must not be allowed to teach.

He believed that a woman's state was lower than that of a *slave*.

The reason he gave for that conclusion is hair-raising. A slave could be made free, but "woman is in subjection by nature." A slave is not.*

We see here the hand of Jerome. By now, no one was allowed to read the Bible except in Jerome's Latin Vulgate. Aquinas was therefore dependent on the woman-hater Jerome for his translation.**

WITCHING TIME

It was the writings of Aquinas which laid a foundation upon which the witch craze later emerged. This means that for five hundred years, the burning of women as witches touched virtually all Europe at one time or another.

THE AGE OF THE WITCH HUNT

Volumes have been written on this era of madness. This era ebbed and flowed throughout all the Middle Ages (1200-1700). Witch hunting would become popular in one country, then recede and re-emerge in another.

---

*Note that these *un*married, single monks, with their unfulfilled sexual drives, blamed their biological fire not on their biology but upon women!

**It would not be until 1520 that a man named Erasmus again gave the world a Greek New Testament. From 400 A.D. until Erasmus, the New Testament in its original language ceased being used. Throughout those years, the Scripture was prohibited from being in any language other than Latin.

The victims were mostly widows and single women. If you were a single woman with a cat or you healed people with herbs, you were a prime candidate for a burning.

Enter Pope Urbane II who declared that the wives of priests (a dying but not dead practice of priests who married) could be sold into slavery! Some of these wives were publicly whipped while others were imprisoned.

Reader, nerve thyself!

Pope Innocence III in 1139 annulled all marriages of priests. These women were classified as concubines— not wives. A small army of priests then marched across Europe condemning the evils of sex for priests. One of them stated:

> The wickedness of women is greater than all other wickedness. . . . A dragon is more curable than the familiarity of a woman. Avoid them like poisonous animals.

(Such are the roots of women's second-class citizenship in God's kingdom.)

This view of women spawned all sorts of further hazards. In 1322, a synod (a gathering of high clergymen) forbade women to be buried in church cemeteries. Only men could have such burials.

It became common knowledge that a man who looked on a woman with lust was being lured by demonic power, a power possessed by women.

It could not get worse . . . could it? It did!! *Much* worse!!

THE BOOK THAT MURDERED WOMEN

Then came Jakob Sprenger's book *The Hammer of Witches.* It was one of the most popular books of that era.

The book was about witches, witchcraft, and women! In effect, the book was an attack on womanhood. In it Sprenger described the kind of unbelievable torture that a woman who was a witch was to be subject to. Witches were demonic. Women in general were evil.

The outcome: the unutterable torture of women and the death of one million women! A million women, tried for heresy or witchcraft, burned alive at the stake.

Gentlemen, you who tell a woman to be silent in a church gathering . . . you who say women are inferior . . . you who place a mountain of rules and regulations on her, I say to you: Look at the company you keep!

Ladies, you have now seen the root and source of your second-class citizenship in the church.

To my fellow men I add: You might wisely look at your favorite Bible passages that suppress women. I suggest you attempt to find an alternate interpretation of these passages. You will certainly be closer to accuracy than the more widely accepted renditions of these passages. There is a great deal to be said in favor of not holding onto your present narrow view.

We come now to the Age of Enlightenment, followed by the Protestant Reformation.

Did things get better for women in the age of our heroes the vaunted Reformers?

Make a guess, for here comes the answer.

Six

The Reformers

Martin Luther (1483-1546) was a child of the age in which he lived. The cloak of the Dark Ages still cast its shadow over the thinking of men. The idea that a woman was inferior to men and that she was evil was still embedded deep in the minds of the Reformers.

Luther rejected the idea of equality between men and women. He excluded women from leadership in the church.

He held women responsible for the Fall. He also said, "Woman is much more liable to superstition and occultism than is man."

In June of 1525, Luther married a remarkable woman named Katherine von Bora. In some of Luther's more obscure writings, you will find him saying: "When Kate gives me trouble I give her ears a good boxing."

Enter John Calvin (1509-1564).

Will all Presbyterians please forgive me, but John Calvin was as mean as a man can get. Further, as a child of the medieval church, Calvin was committed to the views of the church fathers. Here are some of his teachings:

> Let the woman be satisfied with the state of her
> subjection and that she is made inferior to the

more distinguished sex. Because she receives her origin from man she is therefore inferior in rank. She was created for man, therefore she is subject to man. All women are born that they may acknowledge themselves as inferior . . . to the male.

Calvin strongly believed that God governed the earth by delegating authority *only* to men.

Be advised that the step-child of this teaching (only man has authority) has come down to us in the form of the tyranny of elders and/or the overriding power of ministers.

Ministers demanded that God's people submit to them in every way because, according to Calvin, the ministers were submitting to God.

(Even today, many ministers demand that God's people submit to them because they in turn submit to God.)

Was Calvin as mean as history says he was?

You decide.*

What shall we say of his era? Simply this: the Reformers perpetuated the concept that women were second-class citizens in God's house.

Will this mindset ever disappear?

Not likely. Given the trend of history, those who stand for woman's equality will be people who are moving against the tide.

---

* Calvin had his own daughter killed because she did something that, in his mind, made her worthy of death. If you would like to discover the more sinister side of Calvin, you will want to read Will Durant's assessment of Calvin in his volume entitled *The Reformation* (Pages 459-487).

THE EXCEPTIONS

Thankfully, it was during the Reformation that some did appear who moved against the tide. The Anabaptists took a high view of women, not so much in teaching as in practice.

Did it last?

The next time you see an Amish group, you might want to observe the place of the women among them.* The Amish are a branch of the Anabaptists and once held a more liberal view of women.

This battle for women's equality will have to be waged anew in every succeeding generation.

We now move into the Elizabethan Age. Here comes a man as anti-woman as Jerome.

His name?

King James.

Herein lies a tale you are not likely to have heard.

---

* The Amish are descendants of the Anabaptists.

Seven

King James, the Man Who Has a Bible Named after Him

Did you know that King James, of the King James Bible, wrote a book against women? Actually, King James wrote a book about *witches*.

When James King of Scotland ascended the throne of England, he ordered a new translation of the Bible. James was an out-and-out woman hater. Consequently, he followed the same leanings as Jerome. The men who translated the King James Version of the Bible were under the eye of a man who wanted to keep women subjugated.

James took the place of Elizabeth I. He faced four major challenges:

1. to please the Puritans
2. to please the Catholics
3. to please the Church of England
4. to oppose the pesky Anabaptists, who among other things, believed women were equal to men in the church.

Most of all, James needed to make sure the recently founded Church of England gained acceptance. (That was his major reason for ordering a new Bible. He wanted a Bible that leaned toward bishops and clergy.)

His second reason: to insure that translators kept women in their place. As one author observed, James had another goal,

He succeeded infamously at both.

Here are his own words:

> To make women learned and to make a fox tame
> work out to the same end. Educating a woman
> or a fox simply makes them more cunning.

James's entire reign was anti-women. He was so obsessed with the subjugation of women that he wrote a dissertation on *daemonologie,* taking a strong stand for the execution of women who had been convicted of witchcraft.

And what was proof of being a witch, according to King James? James decreed that *hearsay* was enough to establish guilt. This view passed right over the entire process of English justice.

(The influence of his book had a great bearing on the witch hangings of Massachusetts years later.)

James believed that women were susceptible to the devil more than men. He agreed with his contemporary, Joseph Swetenam, who said, "women spring from the devil."

And yes, King James's view of women influenced the King James Version of the Bible and virtually all succeeding versions.*

He cheated: According to the original Greek (in all cases but one), Priscilla and Aquila are spoken of in this order: Priscilla *and* Aquila. But the King James Version reversed that order in Acts 18:26, putting Priscilla second.

---

* Unfortunately, the King James Version has influenced the American Standard Bible, the New International Version of the Bible, the New American Standard Bible, and the Revised Standard Bible and, tragically, virtually every other popular translation of the New Testament in existence.

James's version translates the Greek word *hesvchia* (I Timothy 2:11) as "let the women learn in *silence*." But in II Thessalonians 3:12, the same word is translated correctly, "with quietness." James's translators elected to use "in quietness" when it was a general statement and "in silence" when it referred to women. In such a translation, man could be *quiet* while women had to be *silent*.

This is blind prejudice.

Next.

In the translation of the Greek word *diakonos, diakonos* is transliterated "deacon" throughout most of the New Testament. But when it comes to Phoebe, the woman mentioned by Paul in Romans, translators turned the word into "servant."

The King James Version of the New Testament is top-heavy with discriminations against women. Future translators please take note—we need an honest Greek translation of the New Testament. It follows that it will not be anti-womanhood.

So, we see that throughout history the deck has been stacked against women.

We need a revolution in history. We also need a revolution in the way we translate, arrange and publish the New Testament, not to mention a revolution in perspective and attitude.

We come to the end of this grisly record of the treatment women in history.

Now enters a revolutionist. And to think he started out as a local peasant.

PART III

A Revolutionist
Named Jesus!

Eight

A Revolutionist for Women's Liberty

We come, at last, to light.

There is no way to adequately explain how radical Jesus was in His emancipation of women. Everything about Christ's visit to earth is contrary to all the ways of men.

Jesus was born and grew up in a man's world. Long before Bethlehem, however, He pre-existed. That pre-existence was in another realm, not ours. In realms unseen He was driven to have a counterpart.

In the Talmud and in Jewish proverbs, you can find the following Jewish views of women:

> • Let the words of the Law be burned rather than women be allowed to learn it.
> • If a man teaches his daughter the Law it is as though he taught her lewdness.
> • The woman is in all things inferior to man. Let her therefore be submissive.
> • Let a curse come upon the man who must have his wife or children say grace for him.
> • It is good for that man whose children are male. It is ill for that man whose children are female.

- At the birth of a boy everyone is joyful, but at the birth of a girl everyone is sad.
- When a boy-child comes into the world, peace comes into the world. When a girl-child comes into the world, *nothing* comes!
- Even the most virtuous of women is a witch.

The Hebrews, it seems, outdid the Greeks.

In the temple in Jerusalem (built by Herod and Jewish religious leaders), women were confined to an area called the Court of the Women, which was fifteen steps lower than the court designated for Jewish men. There were no such courts to divide men and women in the tabernacle in the wilderness, nor in Solomon's Temple.

Are we seeing the degrading of women over time?

Then Jesus came!

Jesus Christ walked into that religious, male-dominated world and ripped it to shreds.

He brought the liberating *good news* which was aimed at loving the oppressed and setting them free, including women! Jesus never uttered a negative word about women.

The men around Him were shocked to see Him talk to women! He taught women. He allowed women to travel with Him! He treated women as equal with men. In effect, Jesus Christ tore down the social conventions concerning women, things which had stood for time immemorial.

No man in all of human history was ever as radical in his treatment toward women as was Jesus.

In all this, never forget, the Lord's heart toward women was a reflection of His Father's heart toward women. Thank God this was later reflected in the changed lives of His apostles. You can see the change in their lives in what they later wrote. Jesus Christ had a scandalous birth, and it involved a woman. It took extreme courage for the apostles to tell the story of the Lord's birth.

It would not hurt to see more such courage.

His Birth

Two of the writers of the four Gospels begin their narrative of Christ by telling of the virgin birth of Jesus Christ.

This is scandalous beyond words. In fact, if anyone wrote a biography of any man and started it with the story of the man's virgin birth, we would think him mad and illegitimate. So it was also then!

To call Mary a virgin and at the same time say that she bore a child was the equivalent of saying that she was a fornicator. And yet, Matthew and Luke took a deep breath and recorded the story knowing that first-century readers would be shocked at what they read. That story would be perceived as an admission that she had sex before she was married. The Hebrew mind could not separate these two thoughts.

At a Tomb

Then there was the *end* of the Lord's life on earth. The end was just as scandalous as was the beginning.

It was a *woman* who first reported that Jesus had risen from the dead. In that day, anything a woman might report was considered hysteria.

And then there were the mid-years of His life. Take another deep breath.

AT A SAMARITAN WELL

Unquestionably the most scandalous story ever told in ancient literature was the story of Jesus and the woman at the well. It is also one of the most touching stories in the New Testament. Here is a man starting out from Jerusalem who deliberately routes His way through Samaria . . . even when other routes would have been quicker. To even *go* through Samaria was not something a devout Jew would ever consider. The racial prejudice between Jews and Samaritans was unbreachable.

Jesus sat, *alone*, waiting for His disciples to return from going into town. Deliberately He waited. A Samaritan woman appeared. She ignored Him. She began to draw water from Jacob's well. This woman was so defamed in reputation—even among Samaritans—that she came alone, at a time when all others were sleeping. She was a social outcast even among half-breeds.

He spoke.

She was *shocked* that Jesus would speak to her. This was unthinkable. A man, talking to a woman in public, alone, just did not happen. But it was even more unthinkable that a *Jewish* man would talk with a Samaritan woman. And alone.

What is more, *this* woman was a divorcee!

THE DIVORCED

I speak now to every divorced woman reading this book. Jesus Christ went out of His way to speak to a divorcee.

(One that had been divorced *five* times!) There is hardly a divorced woman alive who does not feel that she is somewhat a second-class citizen.

Jesus held no such view.

Antagonism toward divorcees—male or female—is so much a part of the modern mentality that it is virtually impossible to extract.

Then Jesus came.

He seems to be almost the only Christian "minister" with such openness toward the divorced.

But there is more.

Jesus was not only talking to a divorcee, He was talking to a woman living in adultery.

We can assume from this story that this woman must have been extremely difficult to get along with. (She was married and divorced five times!) To avoid the issue of divorce, Bible scholars have proposed that all of her husbands *died*. (If that is true, then it is even more frightening! Just how, pray tell, did so many men die?) She was now living in sin. She probably did not love the man with whom she was living, nor he her. Her relationship to him was simply her way of getting food and a place to sleep.

The woman at the well was the least likely candidate for conversion in all the first-century story. A much-hated, no longer young, hard-to-get-along-with, multi-divorced adulteress, and a despised *Samaritan*.

From her part of the conversation we deduce that she was also shallow—but not too shallow to show contempt for a Jew who needed a drink of water. This woman who was so far down the social ladder that there was no other step on that ladder still openly declared her disdain for a Hebrew.

It gets more dramatic still.

For a man to speak to a woman publicly—to carry on even the briefest conversation with any woman in public—was tantamount to being evidence of committing adultery with that woman. People were so suspect of womanhood that to speak to a woman was indication that you had slept, or were intending to sleep, with her. The only possible reason any man spoke to any woman was to arrange for sex with her. It was that bad!

Pause and realize it was to *this* woman that Jesus Christ revealed the ultimate truth of the eternals: *God* is an indwelling Lord!

Further, the living God—the Father Himself—was seeking that woman.

It was Jesus Christ's own Father who spoke to Him and told Him to seek out that benighted soul. He wanted to meet her and deliver her. He desired to make her a biological daughter of God.

> The hour comes and it has arrived, right now, when He will be worshipped in spirit . . . and right now the Father is *seeking* those who worship Him in spirit!

Consider this: God put His Son on a circuitous journey to tell a tragic-ridden woman that Jesus Christ was Living Water, that the Water lived inside her, and the day had come when men would worship God no longer in stone buildings, but rather, those who belong to the Lord would worship within their innermost beings.

44

This story has to be one of the most beautiful stories in the history of literature.

THE TWELVE

The twelve disciples were stunned . . . shocked . . . dismayed . . . when they saw that Jesus had spoken to this Samaritan woman. Remember, this is God doing this. Let men wonder at it all. Later, the men themselves changed. After all, John included this shocking story in his Gospel. Yes, the apostles changed. They changed even to the point of saying "the women of our company" (Luke 24:22).

A virgin brought Jesus Christ into the world. Jesus Christ proclaimed some of the greatest truths He ever brought forth on this earth to a five-time divorced adulteress. And Jesus Christ chose a woman to proclaim His resurrection (John 20:10-18)!

You do not get more radical than this.

THE ADULTERESS

If that is not enough, consider the story in which a woman is dragged into the Lord's presence (John 8:3) because she was caught in the act of adultery. All He did was tell her not to do it again.

The first question any of us *should* ask is: "In that story, where is the man she was having sex with?" *Both* were caught in the act.

This woman was brought before Jesus, supposedly to be stoned according to Mosaic law. (The man was also supposed to be stoned, but stoning the man had nothing to do with adultery.

45

He was supposed to be stoned for trespassing on another man's *property*.)

HEAVEN'S VIEW

Take a head-on look at the value system of heaven. Not man's, but God's.

Jesus blew the circuitry of every man when, on two occasions, He spoke to adulterous women, in public.

The primary reason for the subjugation of women (at least by religious men) is men's frustration with their own sex drive. Religious men unconsciously believe that their temptation to lust is exclusively coming from the woman, not the man. The solution: remove women, banish women from men's sight. (Or, in our time, put women in flour sack dresses.)

Then Jesus came!

Jesus Christ, the citizen of heaven and God in-carnate, championed women, even a woman who was caught in adultery! In so doing He addressed the core issue of women's subjugation.

Let us paraphrase what Jesus said.

> Let the man who has never committed adultery,
> never had sex with a woman other than his wife,
> or never lusted after a woman be the man who
> finds fault with this woman.

No such man was present.

The man who dropped the first stone was likely a man who had been with someone other than his wife, while the last man to drop a stone was a young, naïve boy who was yet to fight the lifelong battle of desire.

In that day, women could not divorce their husbands; only a man could divorce his wife. Further, he could do it on a whim.

Then Jesus came.

When Jesus addressed the subject of marriage and divorce (Mark 10:2-12), He rejected this inequality and lifted marriage to the point of mutuality. He leveled the playing field.

But this is not all the Son of God did. Consider these eye openers.

HIS PARABLES

In His parables the Lord also gave honor to women.

In the parable about the woman and her lost coin, Jesus used the imagery of a woman to give us a clearer portrait of *God as Savior* (Luke 15:8-10)! This is one of three parables, including the parable of the prodigal son which illustrates the love of God the Father.

Jesus expressed His feelings toward Jerusalem using the imagery of a female. He spoke of a mother hen spreading her wings over her tiny chicks (Matthew 23:37; Luke 13:34). Here is a female (a hen) being used to illustrate God. The mother hen was a reference to *God Himself.* Look again! Here in this parable, women *bear the image of God.*

On one occasion someone said to the Lord, "Your mother and your brothers are here. They want to talk to you." Jesus replied, "My mother and my brothers are those who hear God's word and practice it." Take note of the depth of these words. Jesus made clear that both females and males who believe on Him become His own kin (Luke 8:19-21). In salvation, the

Son of God equaled women with men.

Let us go now to the village of Bethany and review the famous story of Mary and Martha.

MARY, A WOMAN, IS BEING TAUGHT

First, Mary is allowed to sit at the feet of Jesus Christ. This was socially unthinkable! Second, Martha *complained* to a *man*! Again, unthinkable. And further, she complained in *public*. She went to the top with her complaint. She complained to God!

In allowing Mary to sit as His feet while Martha was tending to kitchen duties, Jesus was liberating women from being limited to the drudgeries confined to their gender. Jesus allowed Mary to leave the kitchen and to be placed in the position of a *disciple*!

A woman in the midst of men. A woman *learning* the *law*! This was forbidden. Mary sat at the Lord's feet, just as did the Twelve. In so doing, He thus numbered Mary among His disciples. That must have blown the minds of all the men who first read this story. A woman was at the Lord's feet rather than fulfilling her *womanly* chores. Further, she had "made the better choice." That could not be comprehended . . . yet here was *God's* view of women.

Never forget, here is the scandal of scandals, Jesus taught a woman! No man with any character or integrity would ever engage in such a thing.

Then Jesus came!

Jesus Christ related to women as human beings, not as cattle, not as property. If you can understand, He did not relate to women as women, but as human beings! In fact, a careful look at the Gospels shows that Jesus always treated women as though they were people, just as were men.

The story of the woman who gave one-tenth of a penny illustrates how highly Jesus viewed women when it came to God's heart about stewardship (Mark 12:41-44).

Again, no critical word of women ever came from His lips.

The Syrophoenecian

Further, Jesus did not restrict His ministry to women who were within the Jewish family. For a Jew to reach out to a non-Jew was unthinkable. On the contrary, He reached out to a Samaritan woman, a Canaanite woman, and a Syrophoenecian woman.*

The Greatest Scandal of Them All

Then, of course, there is Mary Magdalene.

So much can be said of this woman, but there is one thing about her that is often overlooked.

Mary Magdalene followed Jesus everywhere He went. She appointed herself as protector from men who demanded too much of Jesus. When Jesus was tired, she "shooed" people away. When it was time for Him to eat, or time for Him to rest, she was there!

---

* Perhaps the most amazing aspect is that men dared tell these stories, especially the story of the woman who anointed Jesus' feet. The men who were present in that room that evening were mortified at what they saw! For a woman to touch a man, let alone to anoint His feet with oil was beyond unthinkable. What a shock second-century readers had when they read this story. Add to that, this woman had just recently been demon possessed.

As you read the Gospel accounts concerning women, one thing becomes obvious. Jesus Christ was comfortable with women and they were comfortable with Him.

What an incredible man! Jesus was a revolutionist, a revolutionist of the highest order, and most especially so when it came to women. When the common view of women was that they were little more than chattel and their chief purpose was to give men sex and children, Jesus came. Jesus raised women to a level of both dignity and worth.

The fact that the men who wrote the Gospels were so open about what Jesus said and did concerning women shows that these men had also been transformed . . . transformed by Jesus' heart for womanhood.

Jesus not only spoke to women in public, He not only taught women, He not only allowed Himself to be touched by a woman (scandalous), He allowed a woman to touch Him who was, according to Jewish law, unclean (Matthew 9:20-22)!

Still more shocking, He allowed women who were the worst of sinners to touch Him (Luke 7:36-50).

Just as dumbfounding, He chose as His closest friends three women: Mary, Martha, and Mary Magdalene (and let us not forget Joanna). In short, our Lord moved women out of the shadowy world of "they are only for sex" to a place equal with men. He never even came remotely close to the concept that women are the source of sin and sexual temptation.

Does this not touch you? Are you not impressed with your Lord?

Then, gentlemen, you who are called to the Lord's work, you are to be revolutionists! The church still needs revolutionary men. This revolution must be reignited in every generation to come!

FINANCED BY WOMEN

Perhaps one of the most overlooked aspects of the Gospel account is that Jesus was financed by women. Many think of the Lord as someone who had no financial needs. But that is not true. Women always traveled with Jesus, and they were His main financial supporters (Luke 8:1-3; Matthew 27:55,56; Mark 15:40,41).

RESURRECTION

The honor that Jesus bestowed upon women was unprecedented. His greatest display of honor was that He chose to appear *first* to women (not to men) after His resurrection. Thought above all thoughts!

Jesus Christ was making obvious to His disciples and to us all that He was bringing forth a new order on the earth, but an order not of this planet. It was an order that already existed, before creation—one that existed in another realm. That realm tells us the mind of God the Father. To see how Jesus treated women is to understand what *God* thinks of women.*

Those of you who use these passages out of I Corinthians to throw women back into the Dark Ages, best you revisit God's

---

* Among those who followed Jesus in the days of His flesh, there were four who stood at the foot of His cross: Mary the mother of Jesus, Mary (the wife of Clopas), Salome, and Mary Magdalene. These were all Galilean women. They had followed Him to Jerusalem and to a cross; and they were there in Jerusalem after the Lord's death and resurrection.

mind and His Son's mind.

But what happened after the Lord's ascension?

In the time of Pentecost and the period immediately thereafter, did the subjugation of Christian women get lost, or did it live on?

Our story begins in May of A.D. 30. What was the place of women in the first seventeen years of the church?

Go now to Pentecost. One hundred and twenty people are present.

You who would silence women, tread carefully!

Note: What you will be reading next are the events which took place with Christian women from May A.D. 30 on to summer A.D. 47. All those events will be brought to you chronologically . . . that is, in the order of the events.

PART IV

The Amazing Place of Women
in the
Earliest Days of the Church
(Pentecost A.D. 30 to 47—the First Seventeen Years)

On the Day of Pentecost, Peter stood up and said to the waiting throng: "This is the fulfillment of the prophecy of Joel. In the last days I will pour out my Spirit and your sons shall prophesy, but your daughters shall remain silent."

Is there something wrong with this quotation?

Let us see.

Nine

Women in the Church
from A.D. 30 to 47

On Sunday, May 29, A.D. 30, one hundred and twenty men *and* women were meeting together in a second-floor room, praying together as the Lord had instructed them.

So came the birth of the church of Jesus Christ.

Here you have an expression of post-resurrection life, even post-ascension life. Here is divine life expressing itself. Women are squarely in the middle of the activity of God on earth (Acts 1:14; Acts 2:1-4).

From this moment on, the influence of Jesus Christ upon womanhood will remain high and unchallenged.

This was not Jewish. No second-class citizenship here. Here we can find the answer to the questions, "Can women prophesy? And can women pray in public and in the church?" The Day of Pentecost forever settled that question.

It was not just that only men spoke in other languages, but also the women. And the endowment of power included *women*.

Everything that happened on the Day of Pentecost was shared by both men and women.

Simon Peter announced the fulfillment of an ancient prophecy.

> "In the last days," said God, "I will pour out my Spirit on all people. Your sons and daughters shall prophesy" (Acts 2:16,17 and Joel 2:28,29).

Women also received the same (so-called) Great Commission.* Male and female would be going out to Jerusalem, Judea, and Samaria, and the rest of the world.

Women were present and accounted for on every level and fully functioning. Women were there at the birth of the church.

Without any qualification, Luke (the author of the book of Acts) tells us that men and women were full of the Holy Spirit and preached the word of God with boldness (Acts 4:23-31). And women stayed at the center for all the rest of the century.

Joel, Peter and Luke witness to woman's prophetic place.

Women were present when He was crucified, present at the Resurrection, and in the center of Pentecost. Anyone want to bring to question Joel, Peter and Luke concerning women being able to prophesy?

Nor is that all.

ENTER PERSECUTION

Enter the persecutor (A.D. 37).

When Saul of Tarsus began persecuting the church in Jerusalem, believers of both genders were tried, beaten and imprisoned. It is implied that some died.

In the eyes of the persecutors, Christian women were just as dangerous as Christian men!

Then there is the sister of Barnabas, named Mary. The church met in her home. She had servants. (It is likely she was with Barnabas in the selling of everything they owned.) Peter had come to this home in an earlier persecution and jail break.

---

* This was not at all a commission. It was a prediction.

Years later (when Paul brought the eight men whom he had trained in Ephesus all the way to Jerusalem), Mary's home was one of the places where the church gathered.

This brings us up to the year A.D. 47.

Now the pages change. From this point on, the focus of the story will be on Paul's ministry.

We are drawing near to I Corinthians Eleven and Fourteen, Ephesians Five and I Timothy Two. But before we get there, already we sense there is something wrong with the translation of those passages! As we will see, in Paul's early ministry he was as much a champion of women as were the Twelve. In the light that shines in this next chapter there must come the necessity of rethinking what we have been told about Paul. And remember, from this point on we are in the Greek world . . . the great women haters of the Western world.

What shall we find?

PART V

Women in the Church
Outside Israel

Ten

Women in the Church
from A.D. 47 to 50

ENTERING THE WORLD OF THE GENTILES

The overlooked years of Paul's ministry.

Here we meet Paul before he wrote *anything*.

Paul (with Barnabas) entered a region called Galatia.

Four churches were planted, Gentile churches!

Then! Some very legalistic men from Jerusalem came to Galatia and tried to have the Gentile Christians in those churches to undergo circumcision. Paul wrote a scathing letter to these Galatians about what he thought of those men and their legalism. There is one sentence in that letter that is the most audacious and revolutionary statement about man-woman relationships ever written! No one has topped it yet.

Paul told those naïve Galatians that they did not belong to the old creation, but are a new species.

You belong to a new creation. You are biologically different from others, and that means you have a totally different set of values.

In this new species, in this new creation, in God's eyes, you are only one person, not two.

IN CHRIST THERE IS NEITHER
MALE NOR FEMALE.

That statement alone is evidence enough to end forever any question about women's having equality with men in the kingdom of God.

(Maybe, just maybe, Paul has been unjustly and incorrectly accused of chauvinism.)

Ah! But as wonderful as Paul's statement is, there are men who have figured out a way around this statement. This, they say, is what he really meant: "Yes, *in Christ* there is no difference between male and female. *But* in the assembly (the church), there is a great deal of difference!"

So we have to ask this question. Was Paul speaking theoretically or was he speaking practically (Galatians 3:28)?

Draw your own conclusion. But this might help: What Paul said was a statement made in a *church* to a *church*! Paul made that disclosure—there is neither male nor female—*to* a church.

If I am part of an utterly new biological species where there is no difference between genders, does it not affect how I view women? And how I treat women?

Are women equal with men only in God's eyes? When I walk into a living room to meet with my brothers and sisters, are the women in an inferior role? Suddenly, just by entering that room, do men become superior to women?

If I am a new species, then I am a new species, no matter where I walk.

Paul's statement (Galatians 3:28) is the most radical statement about womanhood ever made in either the New or Old Testament! Was this statement just a theory for Paul? Was it just a theological statement without any practical application? Was his word simply hyperbole?

But most of all:

Does Paul's life and practice back up those radical words?

Let us see.

At last we come to Paul's letters. We will look at Paul's letters in the order in which he wrote them. That means we will begin with Galatians, not Romans.*

---

* Check in your Bible dictionary for the date each letter was written.

Eleven

A City Called Philippi in the Land of Those Chauvinist Greeks!

Paul is on his second church planting journey (A.D. 49-52). Silas is with him. Paul and Silas eventually enter the Greek city of Philippi. This is the center of the greatest chauvinists in all the West.

Because of an edict of Emperor Claudius, there were no Jews in the city of Philippi.*

When Paul arrived in Philippi, he did find a group of "God-fearers," *all* women!

Here is an interesting question: Did a woman ever match wills with Paul and win? The answer is *yes*! You can read it for yourself in Acts 16:11-15. Luke tells us that in Philippi a woman named Lydia was so strong-willed that there was nothing that Paul could say or do to prevent that woman from having her way. She won, no contest. Luke, Silas and Paul had to take up residence in Lydia's home!

Furthermore, the assembly in Philippi was born as an all-woman church!

Now, I ask you, did the following happen:

The women all covered their heads, none of them prayed,

---

*See *The Titus Diary*.

none of them spoke? They all kept silent? Not a word was uttered?

Now how could that be an assembly of God? If they could not function, how could there be a church? (Hand signing had not yet been invented.) These women were singing, praying and sharing even before Paul met them . . . *before* they were even saved! Paul told them to stop doing that *after* they were saved?

These women also went out into the city and told the men in the community to come hear Paul.

Gentlemen, you who subjugate Christian women, your bucket has a hole in it.

Thirteen years later (A.D. 63), Paul wrote a beautiful letter to that same assembly. And what do we find in that letter? Even with the most prejudiced reading of Philippians, you will still discover that there are two very strong women present in the Philippian assembly, and they are co-workers of Paul.

THESSALONICA – GREECE!

After Paul visited Philippi, he then moved on to Thessalonica (A.D. 51). In Thessalonica Paul preached in the local synagogue. There were women present. Among those women were some of the city's leaders (Acts 17:4).

Of course, after Paul was in Thessalonica for a little while, he told all these leading women to stop leading, stop functioning in a meeting, put veils over their heads, and keep silent.

Hmmm?

Paul and Silas departed the city of Thessalonica and moved on to the mountain resort town of *Berea*. Something unusual happened in this town. The Jewish leaders actually allowed others than the synagogue leaders to have access to the Hebrew scrolls.

As Luke tells us, the people looked through those scrolls to see if Paul was telling the truth.

As a result, many Jews and Gentiles believed. Among them were prominent women of the city. Anyone in leadership in that city would be a great asset in the midst of the persecution of the church.

Please remember that in Acts, Luke went out of his way to tell us that many important women were saved in Thessalonica and many prominent women were saved in Berea (Acts 17:12). As new Christians, basking in the new-found liberty in Christ, were these women then suddenly told not to talk, pray, sing, speak, or preach, but to place veils on their heads? If so, let us hope these women got hold of Paul's letter to the Galatians.

Paul left Berea (September A.D. 51) and moved south to Athens. An assembly was not born in Athens, but several people were converted there. Among them was a *woman* named Damaris.*

Leaving Athens, Paul moved further south and came to the city of Corinth (November 51 A.D.).

Are we at last coming to those infamous chapters in I Corinthians Eleven and Fourteen?

Actually we are not. Paul did not write I Corinthians until five years *after* first arriving in Corinth.

We are about to meet one of the most gifted, capable women in all the history of the early church! And she was a close friend of Paul. In fact, there is no one in all the churches that he so depended upon as this woman.

---

* Tradition tells us she had been a highly educated and prominent hetaira.

Twelve

Priscilla, Paul's
"Right-Hand Man"

Enter Priscilla.

Her husband's name was Aquila. The assembly in Corinth began in *Priscilla's* home. It was a home she owned. After an eighteen-month stay in Corinth, Paul departed Corinth; but when he left, he turned to Priscilla for help. He asked her and Aquila to leave Corinth and travel with him to the great, faraway city of Ephesus.

So it was that Priscilla departed Corinth and went to Ephesus to prepare the way for the next city where Paul would raise up a church. Paul's "John the Baptist" was a woman!

There is no one Paul so trusted and so called to assist him as he did Priscilla when it came to raising up a new church. She moved out of Ephesus and moved to Italy, her native country. Again, she bought a home, this time in Rome . . . on Aventine Hill. Paul turned to a woman to help him plant a church. Furthermore, Paul asked Priscilla to move a total of four times for the sake of new churches. It was Priscilla who opened the door to the founding of three of the greatest Gentile churches of Century One (Corinth, Ephesus, and Rome.) (Of course she wore a doily on her head and never spoke in any gathering!) There is something else she did. She taught a man!

And wisdom is known by its children.

Priscilla Taught!

After Priscilla moved to Ephesus, a traveling philosopher who had become a follower of John the Baptist came to Ephesus.

Enter Apollos.

This Jewish-Greek philosopher-turned-preacher was a master of the Old Testament. Apollos was both a circumcised Jew, a *Hellenistic* Jew, and a traveling Greek philosopher. He had grown up outside the borders. He was also a first-class orator in the tradition of Greek rhetoric.

Now it is one thing to know the Scriptures, and yet another to know Christ. Having never heard of Christ, Apollos needed instruction. Who, then, tutored this awesome new convert? A woman! Priscilla! What did she teach him? She taught him Christ.

May her tribe increase!

Should not this simple fact forever settle the question of whether or not a woman may teach a man?

Of course not!

Someone always comes up with a view to *rescue* their theology, no matter how absurd!

"She taught a man, but not in a church meeting. She taught Apollos in private!"

And wisdom is known by its children.

I would find no greater honor in my life than to sit at the feet of Priscilla in Corinth, in Ephesus and in Rome! If she walked into any assembly of which I was a member, I would quickly ask that we turn the whole gathering over to her and do so as long as she would like.*

It is now time for us to open the letter to Corinth, written in the year A.D. 57, and the much-puzzling *Chapters Eleven and Fourteen.* Bring your veil, you may need it, especially if you live on the *east* side of Corinth.

To understand what Paul said in those two chapters we must . . .

---

* Perhaps you noticed, Paul plainly states in 1 Corinthians Chapter Eleven that women can prophesy in a meeting, while in Chapter Fourteen he states that a woman cannot prophesy in a meeting. In my Bible, as I measure the distance between the two statements, my tape measure tells me that the two statements are only sixteen inches apart.

Ask yourself, in the light of everything that you have seen thus far, which view best "fits" into the context of the New Testament? In the light of the life of Jesus, and past the Day of Pentecost and forward, we have to say that *women can prophesy.*

Thirteen

Meet Corinth!

Corinth in A.D. 57.

Paul was not in Corinth when he wrote to the Corinthians. He was in Ephesus. There in Ephesus he received a letter that had come from Corinth with a long list of questions. So he picked up his pen and began writing to them.

Many of their questions had to do with the cultural and racial mix of that city. Corinth was a Greek city, with a Greek-dominated culture, including the most male-dominated society in the Western world. The Greeks also have the most philosophical and theoretical minds of the West. They love questions, debates and high-brow speculations. They love to listen to oratory. And they love quarreling.

To complicate matters further, there was its unique geography. Corinth was located on an isthmus five miles from the Aegean Sea on the east and six miles from the Adriatic Sea on the west. The Corinthians even built a rail (from the Aegean Sea to the Adriatic Sea), using slaves to haul the boats across the isthmus from one sea to another. (The ruts of that trolley are still visible even to this day.)

And herein lie many of the problems of the church in Corinth.

The right (east) side of the city was populated by Orientals. On the left (west), people in the church were Italians—that is,

Romans. Orientals on the right, Italians on the left side of the city. And Greeks in the middle of the city!

Somewhere in that polyglot there were gatherings of God's people, all in one room, among whom were also Jews. Think what a spectacular mix the church's gatherings looked like: Orientals, Italians, Greeks, Jews trying to resolve their differences, all in the same home!

A Christian disaster was what happened.

Aristotelian-thinking Greeks, hot-headed, hot-blooded Italians, inscrutable Orientals, and dot-every-i-and-cross-every-t Jews. Paul was over in Ephesus seeking to address all this. Some of the questions they sent him were from the Orientals, some were from the Italians, and *some* from the Greeks. But the most pesky questions were from the Jews!

The Hebrews wanted to dot every "i" and cross every "t" when it came to Scripture. And they wanted their cherished Hebrew views to prevail. In fact, all of the people wanted their respective culture, customs and laws to dominate in the church.

And the view of women?

The views about women were as varied as the men in the meeting.

The Greek men told their wives to stay at home—participate in nothing. The wife is not allowed to come near the front door, but she can go as far as the second door in the home where she resides.

Further, the Greeks had strong opinions about women's hair! A woman's head and hair were all deeply rooted in Greek culture. (Excuse the pun!) Alas! The Greeks had *two* practices. Greek women who were *married* kept something on their heads.

The *unmarried* women, on the other hand, kept their heads uncovered. (By this it was known to all that the young lady was not married.)

The Oriental men in the gathering believed that a woman should have the top of her head covered at *all* times.

If that was not enough, there were the conquering Romans. Romans (like all conquerors) *knew* their views were best and, therefore, should be followed. Roman women owned land, conducted business and, in general, were "their own person." This would be doubly true in Corinth, which was a city of business, commerce and trade. The *only* time a Roman woman *ever* covered her hair (head) was when she was at a heathen temple, going through its religious rituals. At all other times, a Roman woman *never* covered her head. If you doubt, there is not one fresco, painting, mosaic, or statue *anywhere* in Roman antiquity depicting a Roman woman with *anything* on her head, except in heathen worship. Her hair was for fashioning, styling and decorating. The Roman woman's attitude about her hair was similar to women's attitude today in Western cultures. Their hair was changed with every month, or week, or day.

Poor Paul!

It was inevitable that a squabble broke out about what a Christian woman in the gathering should wear on her head . . . or not wear on her head.

So you see, I Corinthians 11:3-19 *never* can be understood without context.

Also keep in mind, no other church, anywhere, had this unique problem.

Dear reader, we now come to one of the most misunderstood passages in all of Holy Writ.

PART VI

Paul—Liberator or Chauvinist?
I Corinthians 11 and 14,
Ephesians 5, and I Timothy 2

Fourteen

Another Look at These Pesky Chapters in Paul's Letter

IS HE REALLY A MALE CHAUVINIST?

Was Paul really saying what Jerome claimed Paul said?

No!

As we shall see!

To understand what Paul said, keep in mind that list of questions the Corinthians sent him. In I Corinthians Eleven, Paul is answering their questions. But we do not know the questions! We will never know! It is similar to your listening to one side of a telephone conversation. We can only speculate what is being said in the other half of the conversation. So also it is with that list of questions.

What *is* crystal clear is this: The church was having a fight over the place of women. They had fights about this in the middle of the meetings.

Those questions had in them *the Roman* view of women, *the Greek* view of women, *the Jewish* view of women, and *the Oriental* view of women.

Also note that Paul waited until the very end of his discussion to let loose a bomb. (He finally gives *God's* view. Then and only then did he drop the bomb.)

What he said was: Corinthians, forget your issues. No other churches have this problem.

"I do not have this problem, nor do any of the other churches . . . anywhere."

Let us now look at the notorious passage in Chapter Eleven.

Jerome, King James, you two are about to get exposed. Your translations are ridiculous!

Fifteen

Just Who Has Authority over a Woman's Head . . . You Might be Surprised

Here is where some have found the dress that goes to the floor, sleeves which go to the wrist and a doily or even a bonnet on the head. There is little of anything in this chapter that is adequately communicated. Traditional translations are in error.

So, I invite you to get your New Testament and turn to I Corinthians Chapter Eleven. We are about to take a revolutionary look at this passage.

Paul is speaking to the church in Corinth.

Here is that much-disputed passage. Remember, you are looking at a passage first translated by Jerome.

I want you to understand that Christ is the head of every man and that the man is the head of a woman, and God is the head of Christ (verse 3).

Every man who has *something** on his head when he is praying or prophesying disgraces his head (verse 4).

A woman who has her head uncovered while praying or prophesying disgraces her head. She is the same as a woman whose head is shaved (verse 5).

If a woman does not cover her head, let her have her hair cut

---

* The word in italics was placed there by Jerome! It is not in the original Greek text.

off; but if it is disgraceful for a woman to have her hair cut off or shaved, let her cover her head (verse 6).

A man should not have his head covered, for he is the image and glory of God; but the woman is the glory of man (verse 7).

(What the question was, we do not know; but the answer Paul gave may not indicate his opinion at all, but that he was simply stating the Jewish view. Why so? Because Paul later contradicts that view.)

Man does not originate from woman, but woman from man (verse 8).

Man was not created for the sake of woman, but woman was created for the sake of man (verse 9).

(This again reflects Jewish thinking, and was certainly argued by Greeks, whose view of women was even worse.)

Therefore, a woman ought to have *a symbol of* * authority on her head because of the angels (verse 10).

(Again, this was a Jewish view of God's purpose for women.)

Then Paul breaks in and gives another view, God's view!

However, in the Lord, a woman is not independent of man, nor is man independent of woman (verse 11).

Paul adds more. Much more. (Folks, this is radical.)

Woman originates from man, and so also the man *has his birth* * through the woman. Ultimately all things originate from God (verse 12).

Judge for yourselves:** Is it proper for a woman to pray to God *with her head* *uncovered (verse 13)?

---

*These words are not in original Greek text.

**This is plural. Paul did not say judge for yourself. He is speaking to an entire congregation.

Does not nature teach you that if a man has long hair, it is a dishonor to him (verse 14)?

But if a woman has long hair, is it not a glory to her? Her hair is given to her for a covering (verse 15).

(Those three verses, 13, 14, 15, are strong words. They also represent a strong Jewish view. But is it Paul's view? We will not know because we do not know the question that was asked.)

Try to keep in mind that there was no such thing as punctuation marks in those days. A question had no question mark, and could look like a statement. There were no periods, either, nor were there paragraphs. Even worse, there was no space between sentences. Every word and every letter in a word was jammed up against the next. Neither were there quotation marks. With all these letters so jammed up against one another, man was not able to read silently until the invention of the printing press, when punctuation and paragraphing and separation of words were introduced. Prior to that, all reading was done slowly, laboriously, and out loud.

As a result of all this, it is impossible to tell whether Paul was stating his own view in this passage or quoting another person's stated opinion.

Paul is covering a series of questions asked of him. But what are the questions?

Now we come to a clearing. Paul speaks his mind, and his words are not only clear, but they also nullify *all* their questions. Listen to him as he speaks to four factions in that one church: Jews, Greeks, Romans, Orientals. He sides with none. He nullifies all their disputes. And he also tells them what all the other churches are doing.

If someone is to be argumentative, I hold to no such practice, nor do the other churches of God (verse 16).

Each of you four factions, believe what you want to and practice what you want to, but as for me and all the other churches, we do not have any of these practices! The other churches have never even thought of any of this. Your squabbling is unique.

We tend to overlook the *next* sentence.

I praise you because you remember me in everything (verse 2), but I do not praise you for this squabble over women's hair! When you come together you do not come together for the better, but for the worse (verse 17).

I hear that divisions exist among you when you come together as the ekklesia, and I partly believe it (verse 18)!

This division has arisen so that those who are approved among you may become evident. When a church has a major problem like this—fighting over what a woman wears on her head (!)—it is in these occasions we find out who are the approved ones (verse 19).*

MISTRANSLATIONS

Let us now see some of the mistranslations of this passage.

First, open your Bible to this passage. Then take a pen and cross out the words in italics. Next, look at the sentence that says, "we have no other custom." Cross out "other."

That is not the correct translation.

The words should be "no such" custom rather than "no other" custom.

---

*Some believe verse 19 goes with verse 20, which is about the Lord's Supper. But, there was no crisis over the Lord's Supper. There was no division in the meetings over the Lord's supper. The problem with the Lord's Supper was people getting drunk! Therefore, verse 19 belongs with verse 18.

Suddenly this passage looks totally different. In fact, the whole verse has changed . . . radically.

The passage now says:

You are the only people with all these views, and be ashamed of yourselves for allowing these issues to come into the meetings! And if any of you insist on being contentious about this issue, I want you to know that I do not hold your views, nor do the other churches.

Now we will look at one of those italicized passages.

Remove the italics and you come up with one of the greatest shocks in all Scripture.

Sixteen

Four Views, One Church

Italians wanted their women to keep their heads free from all covering. The Greeks wanted women to cover their hair, if married. Orientals wanted all women to cover their heads.

The feud got into the meetings. As we saw, this is actually an issue confined to just one city on the entire planet.

What would you have done in a situation with such opposing convictions, all held so strongly? What did Paul say?

Paul did not write this passage with you and me in mind. We want precision. He wrote vaguely. I Corinthians Eleven *cannot* be translated with any degree of certainty.

You now have the opportunity to pick from a number of possible interpretations of this passage.

First, we may ask who is the one who is head of the woman? That is, when the word "head" is used, does it *always* refer to the husband, throughout the whole passage? Or is "head" used with several meanings?

You have several choices. Does "head" refer to God? Jesus? Or her husband? Or maybe the church?

Or in one case—almost certainly—the reference would be to both her hair and her own head.

The woman has a head, yes, but the trumpet does not always sound a clear note. Things do get fuzzy. There are *at least* three

91

(maybe *four*, and possibly *five*) interpretations of what comes next. (Someone will be sure that you are wrong, no matter what you choose.)

1. The covering of a woman is her husband. What is over a woman's head is her husband. Simple enough.
2. It is a cloth, and she should wear it at all times.
3. Absolutely not. The cloth must be worn only when she attends meetings of the ekklesia.
4. No, it is not her husband, not a cloth covering, but her hair. A woman should have hair longer than her husband's.

THE CHRISTIAN VIEW

After all this, Paul steps in. Forget the Greek view of woman's origin and her place with man, and forget the Jewish view. Here is God's view.

Paul gives a short answer to all these thoughts and disputes in Corinth. When he does, suddenly he changes everything drastically. Paul vanquishes the Jewish view and the Greek view! The Christian view?

"Paul, is it not true that man is the head of woman? She is inferior because she came out of man?"

Paul ends the debate.

"Woman originated from man, but man also originated from woman." The fact is, all things (man and woman) originate from God" (verses 11,12).

Seventeen

If That Is Not Enough,
Hold Onto Your Pet View

Hold any view you want, but I Corinthians 11:10, properly translated, turns everything upside down.

Do you see three words in italics?

> For this cause ought a woman to have *a symbol of* authority on her head.

Those three words—*a symbol of*—are not in the original text. So, remove "a symbol of." The translation now reads:

"Therefore, the woman ought to have authority on her head."

Now, take a good look at that word "authority." It is not properly translated! This word "authority" needs to be re-translated.

For 1,700 years—because of Jerome—we have been barking up the wrong interpretation.

In the original language, the word which is translated "authority" here has another meaning. The Greek word *exousia* is best translated "having the right" . . . "having the privilege" . . ."having the prerogative" . . . "having the dominion" and . . . "having the jurisdiction."

(Take a deep breath, dear reader, you may need it.)

Now let us read this same passage again.

A woman ought to have the right, the privilege,
the prerogative, the dominion, and the jurisdiction over her head.

Repeat: It is the woman, not the man; and it is not the local customs of Italians, Greeks, Jews or Orientals that decide what is on a woman's head; it is the woman who decides.

This changes everything.

This translation answers the question asked by the Jew, the Italian, the Greek, and the Oriental. The woman—not the man—makes the decision as to what does or does not go on her head.

This also puts Paul in a whole new light.

SUMMING UP

One thing is certain, verses 6-12 need to be re-translated. Among the Greeks there is one teaching, among the Orientals there is another teaching. The Jews' views are stated in verses 6-9.

Man did not originate from woman, but woman
did originate from man. Man was not created
for woman's sake; woman was created for man's
sake.

Verse 10 would sound as though Paul was expressing this; but it is far more likely that Paul is once more quoting Jewish views. It is very unlikely that Paul is offering his own opinion here, because there is a major change in his words in verse 11. Verse 10 should read:

Therefore, a woman should have prerogative over her head. (The rest of verse 10 should read, "Because of the angels, however. . .")*

In verse 11 we have the great

However!

Paul expresses the Lord's view, not man's—neither Jew, Greek, Italian, nor Oriental.

However, woman is not independent of man; man is not independent of woman. Woman originates through man, and man originates through woman. And all things originate from God (verses 11-12).

Here we see a flawless statement of equality. All of us come from God.

Now, what shall we do with verses 13-15?

Is Paul expressing his own opinion about a woman's hair? Is he saying that a woman should not pray if her head is not covered? Covered by what: by God? by her husband? by her hair? or some kind of hat or doily or veil? Or is this statement made by someone who sent Paul that list of questions? Keep in mind that the Corinthians had the list of questions with them, as well

---

* "Because of the angels" should be part of verse eleven and not verse ten. Therefore, verse eleven would read, "However, because of the angels, in the Lord…etc."

as any comments they made when they drew up the questions. Paul knows what was in their letter; the Corinthians know; but we do not know.

Does nature teach us that woman should have long hair? Or was this a statement made by an argumentative Jew or Greek, or perhaps an Oriental?

If Paul is expressing his own opinion in verses 13-15, he does away with his own opinion about this debate in verse 16—and everyone else's opinion. In verse 16, he tells the Corinthians that the subject never even comes up in the other churches. The other churches do not have any teachings about women's hair, and neither does Paul.

It becomes clear that what happened in Corinth was a clash of culture and tradition which had nothing to do with any other church or anything spiritual.

Ladies, do what you wish with you hair!

Paul took his stand. He told the ladies to do whatever they wished to do with the top of their heads.

That should end the debate forever, right?

We still need to deal with "such" and "other."

Paul was just about to go on to his next subject, which was the Lord's Supper, but he had the last word to end this entire fuss.

"You have a problem, Corinth. No such issue like this exists in the other churches. The rest of the churches hold no such view as you do."

Or . . .

Did Paul say, "The rest of the churches have no "other" view than the one in Corinth. Is it "other" or "such"?

The word used in Greek (verse ten) is *toioutos* and always means "such." The word "other" is a mistranslation of the Greek!

So that settles it all. Other churches had no such problem.

But, alas, some see the verse reading, "I have no custom *except* that of a woman covering her head with a veil. This is also true of all the other assemblies in other places."

If you wish to see the verse that way, then do so, but it is not in the Greek. And in so doing you subjugate womanhood.

Alas. Alas. Someone out there has yet another view of this passage! That view is bizarre. Whoever came up with the following interpretation was a man who wanted total control of everyone—be it male or female. This is what he sees in this passage: "There is no custom in any of the other churches in which anyone ever argues about *anything* when it comes to my authority."

What does that mean? It means, no one is allowed to disagree about anything that is contrary to the opinion of the man who is in charge.

(And wisdom is known by its step-children.)

Fact: only Corinth had this problem!

How did Paul resolve the problem?

Ladies, you resolve the problem. You do whatever you want to do with your hair!

We leave this controversy. Further, there should never have been such a controversy. Jerome, for shame.

Now we go to that other infamous chapter in Paul's letter. It is I Corinthians Fourteen.

Ladies you are to be silent and *keep* silent.

Is that true? Or did Paul once more get accused unfairly? Let us see! Actually, the very next page is a good place to start.

Philip had four daughters who prophesied!

—Acts 21:9

Eighteen

Are Women to Be Silent in Church?
(Women Are *Not* to Be Silent)

Jerome's translation states that women should be *silent*. And King James cheated with the Greek language to make it say that women should not speak in a meeting.

And so it is that we come to I Corinthians Fourteen. We have come to a place of battles, bleached bones, and (un)holy wars. Before we cross this treacherous terrain, let me make one observation.

Chapter Thirteen comes before Chapter Fourteen!

(Chapter Thirteen is the beautiful poem of love.)

Chapter Fourteen begins with the sentence, "Pursue love."

(We have not! Not with our abuse of this chapter at least!)

The chapter then says: Desire spiritual gifts, especially prophecy.

Paul wrote this statement—desire spiritual gifts—specifically for men only? Deliberately cutting out women?

Not so! Paul went on to say, "I would like for *everyone* to speak in tongues" (verse five).

Tongues is for everyone, except women?

When Paul states, "You may *all* prophesy, one after another" (verse 31), is he addressing men only?

Dear reader, when Paul makes statements like "you all" or "every one of you," he is speaking to the *entire* church!

That, plus the rest of the New Testament, makes it clear that women spoke in meetings. To attempt to say otherwise would be a feat of scriptural gymnastics. The only place where there is a contrary statement appears to be in verse thirty-four which says: "Women should remain silent in the churches."

But is this Jerome again? And King James?

Or . . .

Is it even imaginable that Paul would tell women in a gathering of the body of Christ that they must never speak? This runs contrary to everything else in the New Testament and certainly bypasses the raucous, loud, out-of-control church gathering in Corinth.

Something therefore is amiss.

And the "amiss" is in that word *silent*.

Try to imagine this: In every church Paul planted, he would tell all the women to be silent. "Say nothing."

What would be the final outcome of such practice?

It would kill a church! It *does*, in fact, kill churches.

Paul never once told women to stay silent in a Christian meeting. If he had wanted women to be silent, he would have used a word that meant "muzzle" or "shut down." That word is *phimoo* (fim-O-oh).

Jesus once answered a question of the Pharisees, and as a result of his answer, the Pharisees were *shut down* by his words (Matthew 22:34). The Pharisees had nothing they could say. Jesus also used the word *phimoo* when He told an unclean spirit to be silent (Mark 1:25).

The Lord Jesus again used the same word when He quieted a raging sea (Mark 4:39). *Phimoo,* then, means *causing someone to be silent.* But, Paul did not use that word in I Corinthians Fourteen.

There is also another word Paul could have used to tell women to be silent. It is *hesuchia* (hey-soo-KEY-a).

But, Paul used neither of these words. Instead, Paul chose the Greek verb *sigao* (sig-ah-o). The word *sigao* means being voluntarily quiet. Jesus also used this word when He asked His disciples not to mention the transfiguration until after His resurrection (Luke 9:36). On another occasion, Jesus said to the Pharisees that if His disciples "became (voluntarily) quiet"—which was something that the Pharisees were demanding—"then the stones would cry out" (Luke 19:40).

Later, when Jesus was on trial before Pilate, He *voluntarily remained* quiet as he stood before Pilate (Mark 14:61).

Then there was the time Paul was telling the Twelve about his first church planting journey. The apostles quietly (*sigao*) listened in awe. This is a perfect example of what Paul meant. The apostles knew how to voluntarily listen *quietly*. These men did not interrupt Paul as he gave his report.

(One can listen quietly, but not necessarily in stone silence.)

Sigao is the perfect word for Paul to use. When there is disorder around . . . *sigao*.

I meet with Christians who meet in homes. In these gatherings, everyone speaks out and once in a while *sigao* is definitely needed.

So, dear reader, there are definitely times, in open meetings, especially, when *sigao* is needed.

Too Much Silence

God's people have now been *silent* in church meetings for the last 1,700 years.

No wonder people would like to say something after 1,700 years of silence.

Now we move to I Corinthians Fourteen, verse thirty-five, which is a really prickly passage. It says it is a shame for a woman to speak in the assembly.

Do we at last meet chauvinism?

Paul had twenty-five words in the Greek language to choose from to convey the word "speak." Those twenty-five words can describe many shades of "speak" and "teach". Five of these twenty-five words imply "proclaiming," "preaching," or other aspects of oratory. Some of the differences in these twenty-five words are so minute that a non-Greek could not possibly grasp the finer difference.* What word did Paul use here? He did not refer to preaching. He did not refer to teaching. He did not refer to proclaiming, giving a discourse, or even an oration. No polemics here, at all.

What Paul said was that women are not to *laleo* (la-LAY-o). *Laleo* is the one word that simply means "talk."

In what circumstance would Paul ask women not to talk?

Let me be contemporary.

Do some situations really fit Paul's words? Yes, and I testify to that fact. Among the churches I work with, I have had to say, on rare occasions, "Hush. In the midst of all our freedom, please would you people not chat."

Informality in a meeting sometimes breeds *chatting*. Is this a "woman" problem? No! Brothers, do the same. If two, or

---

*We are told that the Eskimo language has over one hundred words for snow! Try coming up with one hundred words for snow! The Greek language had twenty-five words for "speak" because, as the Eskimo had so much snow all around, the Greeks were surrounded by oratory.

three, or four (be it men or women) are chatting away, they can pretty well kill a meeting. At the very least, they will be a distraction.

Consequently, for the sake of the meeting and for the sake of the one who is presently sharing about the Lord, please do not chit-chat!

A great deal of today's debate about I Corinthians Fourteen is due to the fact that the people who are doing the debating do not have a first-century atmosphere with which they can identify. In fact, we are usually reading the New Testament with a modern mind-set. Our image of "church" is people sitting in pews all dressed up nicely, all silent, and a pastor preaching to the audience. But our forebearers met in homes, sat on the floor, experienced community, and smelled terrible! Try to overlay that on a Sunday morning gathering in an institutionalized church and you miss the entire context.

What Paul was saying just does not fit anything we do today.

For those who live in the reality of open meetings, these passages do not strike us as strange at all. In fact, they sound like last week's meeting!

Again, to put it in modern terms, Paul was saying to the women who were disrupting the church meetings, "Shhhhh! Dear Christian, I know we have not seen one another for three whole days, and there is much for all of us to talk about. But, will you please start a song, or share, or pray? Please do not start chattering."

Now, are we finally past the difficult passages in Paul's letters? Think you can finally breathe easy? Wait until you read Ephesians Five.

Nineteen

Must a Wife
Submit to Her Husband?

EPHESIANS FIVE

Let me say this as strongly as possible: There is no Scripture that is more abusive to womankind than a passage in Ephesians Five . . . as it is usually translated today.

Let this author go straight to the point.

Submission as stated in Ephesians Chapter Five is not a passage to be delivered by a pastor to a congregation of people the pastor hardly even knows. Sir, there are psychopaths, sociopaths, wife beaters and women haters out there in your Sunday gathering, and some are looking for a Scripture to give them permission to abuse their wives.

Furthermore, there is the *translation* to be considered.

It is not so much a poor translation as it is a blatant invention. The translation is not even there. Here is a perfect example of Jerome creating words which are not there. Words are inserted that are not in the text, and those inserted words radically change the meaning of the passage.

Be clear: This passage is relevant only to people who are living in the matrix of Christian community. That is who this passage was penned to. Paul would never have thought in any other terms. This is not a passage to be applied universally, but only in Christian community with its safeguards automatically built in.

This passage was a statement made by a church planter to a church—to Christians all of whom knew one another. Outside of that context you are in danger of giving license to men abusing women.

Be dogmatic about the passage only if you know all the people in your audience and know them well. The modern church simply does not offer that possibility. You have no idea the strange thoughts of men in a Sunday morning gathering.

Point! Paul's words were not penned to *any* individual. This letter is to a church . . . a body of people.

Today we have a disposition to read the New Testament as though it contained only static truth. We preach out of context. Men teach such passages without even thinking of church life.

Paul taught only in the context of community. He taught only in a church where everyone knew everyone.

Tragedy of all tragedies, we read all of Paul's letters as though everything in his letters was written only for the individual.

A wife *must* submit to her husband? Regardless of the fact this passage was written not to an individual, but to a body of believers? In such a scenario, the woman is not only a second-class Christian, but an *unprotected* woman!

The corporate model of church life is virtually unknown today. But, in the first century, living in community and being the church were one and the same.

Christians sitting on the floor of a living room, in a house which belonged to a man named Philemon in Colossae—that is who this passage was written to. People in that room cared for one another and protected one another. If you were to read Paul's letter *that* way, then Ephesians would become a new book.

And if you do this with all of Paul's letters, you will see Christianity revolutionized.

Dear sister in Christ, do not tolerate a teaching that has no checks and balances. The context concerning "submission" is for community only!

THIS IS NOT WHAT EPHESIANS 5:22 SAYS!

"Wife submit to your husband" is not what the passage says.

Paul said: "Wives (plural) be to your husbands (plural) as unto the Lord."

Look again. Do you see *submit** here in the text, or only in italics?*

Here is what the text actually says.

Wive*s* be to your husband*s* as to the Lord.

"Submit" is in *italics* (thanks to Jerome).

Further, the nature of the text is a corporate word, from a corporate mind, to a corporate mind. Beyond that, note that this passage is Christ-centered, not man-centered. Paul places two *plurals* in this sentence (wive*s*, husband*s*) without even thinking. Rather, Paul was thinking *corporately.* "Wives, be to your husband*s* the same way you would be to the Lord."

Everything has changed. This new meaning is not a harsh word to wives about submission, but a highly Christ-centered observation.

*Some translations use the words "be subject to," but these words are still in italics because they do not appear in the original Greek text.

When Paul spoke of "wives," he involved all the married women of the entire assembly. An abusive husband could not have survived the collective nature of the church in that day. When Paul's letter was read, the hearers sitting in the living room were utterly involved in one another's lives. Any eyes in that room would have fallen on an abusive man long before they fell on an unsubmissive wife!

Today, such body protection is lacking in the traditional church. Again, pastors, there are harsh men out there just waiting to hear this passage, in order to justify their abuse and even brutality!

Ephesians 5:21 tells us that *everyone* is to be subject to *one another*. Here is mutuality. When we lose that mutuality, we also lose balance. This is the only honest way Ephesians 5:21 can be applied.

THREE TO WOMEN, NINE TO MEN

It is often noted that Paul writes only three sentences to speak to the wives (verses 22-24). He writes *nine* sentences to speak to husbands (verses 25-33).

Paul's main concern was that husbands love and cherish their wives . . . just as Christ loves His counterpart!

Always, the final, central word is *Christ*.

"As Christ is the Head of the assembly, the husband is the head of the wife" (verse 23).

Whatever Christ is to the body, *that* is what the husband is to be to his wife.

Sir, are you afraid of Christ in His role as head of the body? Is there any fear in you toward Jesus whatsoever? Is there any terror or any misgiving in your heart, as concerns Christ? Husband, then it is your business to make sure your wife feels that same sense of peace toward you! You cannot accomplish that by insisting on submission. Christ is to be the standard for the husband!

Just what did Christ do? He stepped in and shielded, protected, saved and laid down His life for His bride. His wife is not browbeaten to "be to Christ." The body of Christ comes to "be to Christ" without thinking about it, and certainly is not ordered to do so! How does a man—and more especially a woman—come to acquire this freedom in a way that is truly living and natural and organic? And, women, having laid hold of this freedom, how do you keep it? One thing is certain, it is not by hearing the drumbeat of the traditional recitation of Ephesians Five.

The next time you hear someone's misinterpretation of Ephesians Five, please recall to mind this chapter in this book.

In so doing, be set free.

Now we come to the most anti-woman passage in all of Paul's writing.

But, first let us look at an excerpt of Ephesians Five as translated from the Greek.

This is Ephesians Five 19-24 (written in English) as it appeared originally in Greek without punctuation or paragraphs. I made the first part of the passage easier to read for two reasons: one to help you become used to how to read and second, to realize that the context of the passage is about how to sing in a meeting, *not* about wives submitting to their husbands!

SPEAKINGTOONEANOTHER

INPSALMS

ANDHYMNS

ANDSPIRITUALSONGS

SINGINGANDMAKINGMELODYWITHYOURLORD
ALWAYSGIVINGTHANKSFORALLTHINGSINTHE
NAMEOFOURLORDJESUSCHRISTTOGODTHEFATHER
ANDBESUBJECTTOONEANOTHERINTHEFEAROF
CHRISTWIVESTOYOUROWNHUSBANDSASTOTHE
LORDFORTHEHUSBANDISTHEHEADOFTHEWIFEAS
CHRISTISTHEHEADOFTHEGATHERINGHEHIMSELF
ISTHESAVIOROFTHEBODYBUTASTHEGATHERINGIS
SUBJECTTOCHRISTSOALSOTHEWIVESTHEIRHUS
BANDSINEVERYTHING

Twenty

Can Women Teach Men?
What Does I Timothy,
Chapter Two, Say?

This passage is regarded by many as the most chauvinistic passage in the entire New Testament. We speak of I Timothy 2:9-15. This passage has stopped the heart of many a soul.

CONTEXT NEEDED—VERY MUCH NEEDED

Of all places to accurately understand Paul, it is in I Timothy. Without the context, you will not see Paul in the proper light.

When Paul wrote I Timothy, the land of Israel was being ripped apart by civil war. Further, Israel was on the verge of being invaded by the legions of Rome (A.D. 64-65). The Christians who had once lived in Israel knew the Romans were coming, and they departed Israel *"en masse"*. Some were going south to Africa, many traveled eastward to such places as Transjordan, Persia and Babylon, but most were fleeing north. They had come to places like Asia Minor, Greece, Galatia, and Italy!

The letters to Timothy and Titus, along with a letter by Peter, were written during this exodus. Peter wrote to the Jews who had moved into Galatia and other areas where Paul had planted Gentile churches. Peter told the Jews to respect the local

Gentile elders. But many Gentile churches did not have elders! Paul's two disciples, Timothy and Titus, had not chosen elders in many of these places. Imagine what would happen if Israeli Jews moved to Gentile churches where there were no Gentile elders!

Paul acted. He armed Timothy with a letter. Timothy was to carry this letter to the Gentile churches. The letter would explain what elders were and that Paul had chosen Timothy to select those elders! Timothy, letter in hand, set out to cross Asia Minor and go into the elder-appointing business.

Despite the fact Paul drew up a list of qualifications of an elder, he did not do so for Timothy's sake. Timothy had no need to be told the qualifications of an elder. Timothy had been at Paul's side for almost twenty years! But, in some areas of Asia Minor, the saints seemed virtually clueless as to what an elder was.

It was for this reason Paul told Timothy to have this letter read publicly wherever he went. Paul's letter to Timothy was read out loud!

The letter was written so that each church could see the needs and the solutions of that hour.

Here was a letter written at a time when there was empire-wide confrontation between Israel and the emperor, Nero, with Jewish and Gentile believers caught in the middle.

When Paul penned this letter, he addressed some peculiar problems in specific locales. He also touched on the unique situation of women: married, unmarried, and widowed.

Note this amazing fact: Paul spoke of how women are to receive instruction. That in itself is amazing. Women are being *taught* in I Timothy 2:11-14.

"A woman should quietly receive instruction with entire submissiveness (I Timothy 2:11).

Is Paul the father of Christian education for women?

Then came that terrible statement:

> I do not allow a woman to teach or exercise authority over a man, but rather to remain quiet. After all, it was Adam who was first formed and after Adam, Eve. It was not Adam who was deceived, but the woman was deceived and fell into transgression.

The only thing to do with this passage is to take it at face value.

Does the Greek language help us here?

Yes!

First, Paul did not say, "I do not allow a woman to have authority over a man." Rather, what he said was something even *more* powerful than that. He said, "I do not allow a woman to *dominate* a man."

There is no situation in community living where a people would put up with the domineering of a woman over a man.

I would not.

The church in community will not.

Counterwise, a church in community would not allow the reverse, that is, the domineering of a man over a woman!

Those churches to which Timothy was traveling *were* in community. They were not like today, with Sunday morning meetings where no one knows anyone. (Today most Christians have no idea who the people are who are sitting in the pews around them.)

In community, no one would have to quote Paul for a proof text in order to recognize a practical way to handle such a situation. Be it male or female, domination would somehow be addressed. The sisterhood of a church would not allow it. That is how it would be addressed. Or the brotherhood, or whoever got there first.

Somewhere in a church in Asia Minor, there was a domineering woman who had tried to take over the leadership of a church. Paul was telling Timothy "when you get to that church, do something about that situation! I will help you. I will state my feeling about this." Paul was easing Timothy's job by addressing this problem in the letter beforehand. Remember, the letter was to be read out loud to any church Timothy traveled to.

In order to stress the seriousness of the problem, Paul selected the strongest word in the Greek language. In fact, I Timothy Two is the only place in the entire New Testament where this word is used. The word is *authenteo* (au-then-TEE-o). The word means to dominate . . . or to squash.

Some woman in Asia Minor was seeking to dominate men (2:12) and Paul called for it to end.

This is in the passage about women teaching men, so let us look at the two issues together.

Paul says a woman is not permitted to teach a man. Some see this statement as permanent, everlasting. Is Paul saying, "A woman can *never* teach?" Taking that view, teaching is not open to women. But Paul was not discussing an office or position. He was discussing an activity.

In the Greek, the verb *epitrepo* is written in the *present active tense*. Paul could have written this statement in the *imperative mood*, but he did not. Paul is not saying that women "are not to teach" in a timeless sense. Rather, Paul is referring to a temporary directive. This particular passage has reference to a specific problem in a specific church in Asia Minor.

Let us go further. There is no place in the Greek version of the Old Testament (called the Greek Septuagint), nor anywhere in the New Testament, where the verb *epitrepo* is used in the present active, indicative, first-person singular, except here. This statement is not chiseled in stone. This unique verb structure speaks of something specific, timely and temporary.

Try putting the following in English!

> I do not permit a specific woman to be a teacher—
> not to dominate a specific man in the area of an
> official capacity.

In a specific situation, a woman was teaching. She was unqualified to teach, by reason that she was domineering a man. Timothy was there to put an end to this and to do so at the instruction of Paul.

The problem was not that women were teaching and should not, nor even that a woman was teaching men. Rather, it was that someone was domineering a specific man and therefore had no business teaching.

There are no gender restrictions in I Corinthians 14:26 and Colossians 3:16. And the word which Paul used (*anthropos*) also has no gender connotation.

When Paul spoke about a body of believers exhorting one another in the gathering, he could have used the word *aner*, which would have had specific gender connotation. He did not.

117

If Paul had been making an absolute prohibition of women's teaching men, then how could we ever explain Priscilla's teaching a man (Apollos) who was himself a master of the Scriptures!

Now let us look closely at this matter of women being instructed. In this passage are we looking at something unprecedented and revolutionary concerning women's freedom?

Twenty-One

Women's Education

During those days women were taught not to be taught. Yet, here is Paul speaking about how to instruct a woman. Women were to receive instruction quietly (not silently) and receive it with mutual submission.

The fact that women were being educated was revolutionary. In antiquity a woman's conversation was generally with other women, and that was simply because women were cut off from the wider sphere of knowledge and social exchange.

(The church of your Lord was a forerunner of women's education.)

Exactly who was teaching these women? We do not know, but Paul was telling a group of women who had never been in a teacher/student situation to listen quietly and to listen reverently to the person doing the teaching. No teacher would ask less of either male or female students.

Adam and Eve

The women in the churches in Asia Minor heard this letter, including Paul's words "I do not permit a woman to be domineering of men." Then he gave an explanation of that point. "Adam was first created, then Eve."

Then comes what appears to be a truly strange statement. The woman, not Adam, was seduced. Woman was the first to fall into transgression. Paul is not saying that Adam was not guilty. Look again at that statement. There is nothing positive being said about men. The negative statement is also negative about men.

Woman was seduced, but *man* sinned with full knowledge of what he was doing! The woman was deceived. The man was not deceived. Adam walked into disobedience knowing exactly what he was doing. When he bit into that fruit, he had one goal: to become a god!

Please note that when context is added to these passages, a great deal of light comes with it.

The indictment is not centered on woman, but man!

In the next chapter you are about to hear from Christian women . . . today's women . . . women presently living in freedom and living in the church. I call to the bar the present-day testimony of women living today who are free and equal.

Restore a matrix where church and freedom go together and you will reclaim liberty in Christian womanhood.

Do not say the restoration of your freedom is impossible. There are women living in this freedom, even today.

Now learn how that freedom has been established in other places.

PART VII

Making This Practical

What you are about to read may not be easy to grasp.

The churches which you are about to meet are unique. Therefore, you will find that comparisons are not easy to make. But your spirit will most likely cry "Yes! Why not?"

When women are free in the church, unbelievable creativity appears. Unfortunately, neither the freedom nor the creativity can exist in the framework of the traditional church as it is presently constituted. There must be major changes. Otherwise, what you are about to read cannot be duplicated because of present traditional church settings.

The first thing you must do is to move the chariot of freedom outside its present setting.

How, then, do you go about creating an atmosphere in which women can discover their freedom?

Keep in mind that the present matrix of the church has no place for such overt freedom. Nor is this true just of women, but also of men. To use but one illustration, it is not possible to bring forth an atmosphere of liberation and freedom because of the barrier created by the church building! After all, how can people be set free when they sit in pews with everyone facing in the direction of a man standing in a pulpit?

The women are not free, neither are the men. In fact, *everyone* present is a *mute*. Muteness and freedom are mutually exclusive.

(But what about a regular gathering of women, held in a typical church setting? After all, there are such things!)

Let us imagine such a gathering where women are being taught freedom. It is still a "speaker/listener" format. The women are sitting quietly. The meeting ends, and nothing practical comes out of it. Let us move to the really practical, not the philosophical or theological.

Twenty-Two

First Step Toward Women's Freedom in Church Life

What you are about to read is dangerous. It is dangerous and difficult. Why? Because it cracks the matrix. However, should you dare, it will give new meaning to the term, "like ducks to water."

How to begin having meetings in freedom? Easy. Begin with an all women's meeting. Make sure your first meeting is in a living room. It must be a meeting that is comfortable and informal.

That seems easy enough!

Ah! But it is ingrained in present-day Christianity that there must also be a leader present. On the contrary, one of the people who *must not* be in that room is the pastor or his wife or any other kind of leader.

Remove the leader, any leader. Do not even have a facilitator! Does that not open the meeting to chaos? Yes.

Then is this not dangerous? Yes—very dangerous!

There is one Himalayan fact above all others: Ministry does not trust laity. Preachers do not trust laymen or laywomen. Ministers *really* do not trust women, especially women turned loose without a leader and meeting on their own.

So, you see, this is different. In fact, it is a leap of faith on everyone's part. Yet, freedom is freedom.

129

And yes, women without a leader are trustworthy. Trust them. Ladies, get together leaderless.

Ah, but will not strong women take over?

Yes, bank on it! (I repeat, this is dangerous.) But it is also part of the process. Try to understand that there is a divine indwelling in every woman in that room. If you are willing to gamble for the long haul, you will discover something beautiful and amazing—the emergence of an organic expression of Christian womanhood.

Here is the really best way to begin. Start with fifteen women (ten to twenty) getting together for a sleepover! (No leader present.) I highly recommend a *pillow fight* that night. There can be no religiousness in the room. This is crucially important. A few songs, maybe, but that is all. No messages. No devotionals. Just women *talking*, women *laughing*, women having *fun*, women being women.

Dangerous, difficult, scary, but also fun!

The next time these women get together they will be more relaxed with one another. What do they do then? It really does not matter a great deal, just as long as they are together, being women.

Try this: Have each person tell how she met the Lord. (This could take weeks, and that is great.) This will not only give everyone present an opportunity to tell her story, but it will give the women a long period of just being together and being real people, getting to know one another.

No projects. No programs. No professionals.

Sharing, and no more.

What will eventually emerge? An organic expression of Christian womanhood.

Yes, it will take time before they arrive at such a state. They will probably pass through a number of stages getting there, but it will come . . . if they just keep out leaders!

This is organic womanhood. Let them find it, without help.

There may be one or two people who are impatient. Such a person will surely decide this is all going to fail unless someone steps in. That also gets worked through. How? By divine instincts. By the natural intuitive sense of the women in that room.

I am loath to give away secrets gained over a lifetime, but here is one. At the very beginning, all the women make an agreement that after a few weeks, each one will receive a sheet of paper and pen, and there will be a secret poll taken! All agree beforehand, at the very first meeting, what to expect to find out when the poll is tallied. And after the vote is counted everyone will hear the results and receive it in good humor. All promise that no one will get their feelings hurt . . . or at least will not show it!

All will vote by secret ballot on the following questions:

1. When we get together, who over-functions?
2. Who under-functions?
3. Who talks too long?
4. Who is controlling?

And if you dare:

5. Whose sharing is overly shallow?
6. Who is too "teachey"?

The votes are counted, the results are announced. And in a few months, do it all over again.

Does this help? Does it work?

It works. And, so far, I have never known of anyone being offended.

And more openness follows.

We now move on to resolve some of the stickiest and most unsolvable of problems.

This is not a time to close this book!

Twenty-Three

Women Setting Women Free

Here is the secret of workable, "do-able," equality in church life. But be careful, because from this point on you will have marched off the map.

A LAW OF LIFE

When a group of women are together, invariably they act differently than they do when men are present. Place that beside the law of gravity. When women are together they do not act the same as when men are present.

A group of men together are not like men when women are present. Put a group of men in a room in an informal setting, without any religiosity present and no woman present, and soon there will emerge a very wonderful (and predictable) camaraderie.

The same is true of women (if you leave out the word *predictable)*. Men's "openness" is *never* as open with men as is openness among women. We men are aghast at women's openness with one another. Men would never share anywhere near as openly with other men, even if someone put hot pokers to their feet!

Here, then, are realities. To first set women free, women must gather with women. The same goes for men. Make camaraderie come first.

The Mistake of the Feminist Movement

At this writing there is a so-called feminist movement in the Western world. That movement is rejected, and should be rejected, by the evangelical Christian community. The reason, besides the fact it has no Christian orientation, is that there is a foundational flaw. That flaw is the concept that a woman is the same as a man.

That is not true.

Men are not women, and men are not like women. Women are not men, and women are not like men. Therefore, one of the most important and most powerful acknowledgments is simply this: Women are different than men in a multitude of ways. And Christian women together are a unique species. That difference does not cancel out their freedom or their capacity to be free. In fact, it is the door to freedom.

Being Personal for a Moment

I belong to the house church movement. We meet in homes. We have no leader. (Getting to that point, too, takes a long time!) We have hundreds, if not thousands, of issues and situations and problems that call for the wisdom of God Himself. And it is God to whom we look for that wisdom. Let me hasten to add that among the things that guide us are our past experiences and our failures. Floundering around until we eventually find solutions is our way of life.

How do we get to freedom and equality? By first admitting that, in general, neither gender is really free in a typical church setting.

Religion enslaves.

The first step to freedom is for men to find freedom among men and for women to find their first taste of freedom among women.

So, while the women are having that sleepover (or a few weeks earlier or later) the men go on a weekend camping trip. Again, no particular agenda, just men getting accustomed to being with one another . . . having fun . . . and (to sound the drum once more) with no minister present.

Very soon, even amazingly soon, there grows up an organic relationship among the men. What is it like? The men laugh a lot, they tease a lot. They can move from serious to funny in the blink of an eye. They can move from spiritual to practical even more quickly.

I have heard the men sing the following:*

> Give me some men who are
> Christ-centered men,
> Who will live by the life of their Lord.
> Start me with ten who are
> Christ-centered men,
> And I'll soon give you ten thousand more . . .
> Oh! . . .

*To the tune of *The Vagabond Song*.

135

Shoulder to shoulder, and bolder to bolder,
Together we go to the fore;
Then there's nothing in this world
Can halt this rising tide,
When, stout-hearted men . . .
Stand together side by side!

I have often said that if I cannot go to heaven, please let me go to a brothers meeting.

(Chisel this in stone: There will never be an organic expression of Christian manhood as long as there is a professional religious person in the room.)

There are a few absolutes. The men present must be men who all work for a living. This allows them to be comfortable without the presence of religious professionals.

Women, too, will not share with one another freely with a religious professional present. What is their natural expression? One thing is certain: It is different from men's. Women would never treat women the way men treat men. Once these two unique experiences of freedom are joined, freedom is at the door . . . and what comes out is like nothing else on earth.

The great mistake of people's efforts to establish equality is in trying to introduce democracy. This does not work. You end up with a room full of men not being men and women not being women.

First, you must establish organic Christian womanhood. And you must establish organic Christian manhood. Then put them in the same room and sit back in awe! This author is not going to pursue this further in this book because it will take another book. But I will give you one illustration of what to expect.

Someone in the church was having a very important anniversary. The church, as a whole, decided to put on a play—that is, a full-blown Broadway-like professional play. (It was over two hours long.)

A script was written, without any professional help.

Costumes were made, scenery was created out of thin air, songs were written. Then there was practice, practice, and more practice. All the elements were then brought together to make one complete and beautiful whole.

When they actually staged the play—a musical—it was fantastic. Everyone in attendance cried. It was almost Broadway quality. But here is the amazing part: There was no appointed director. It was brothers; it was sisters . . . in this together.

More amazingly, no one noticed this fact. Impossible, but it happened. No one said "This cannot be done; it would be chaos." (It was, during some stages of the preparation.) It never crossed anyone's mind to say, "We must have a leader."

What happened during those days of creation and preparation was as natural as breathing. The joy, the fun, the chaos, and the absolute creativity—it was all organic.

Point: True freedom is dependent on women finding their "women's type" freedom. And women's freedom is also dependent on men finding their natural "men's type" freedom. Neither, absolutely neither, has freedom until both find freedom. Freedom for women to be women; freedom for men to be men. Then comes a church that walks in freedom.

Men and women express their freedom in different ways. Gender is like that. After that, mutual freedom and its unique gender expression comes to full fruition. How does it look? It cannot be described, but put them all in the same room and watch creativity, joy, and utter uniqueness go through the roof. Yes, sometimes watch the fireworks . . . but most of all, watch the joy.

Christian women find freedom; Christian men find freedom. Then true freedom in the church reigns.

Ask anyone in a traditional church how to achieve total equality in a church, the answer would be, "In a business meeting of the church, let all have an equal say."

Again, this does not bring about equality and freedom in the church. What you will have is a secular democracy. Equality does not mean democracy, and democracy does not equal freedom . . . not in the kingdom of God. Let men find freedom, let women find freedom; then put them in a room together, and the women will keep being women and the men will keep being men. And the meeting will be worth buying tickets to see it.

By this time, women will be perfectly free to be themselves with men in the meeting, and even with religious overseers present. (But I would not recommend the latter.)

There are three separate ways Christians function:

1. Men function in a meeting with men.
2. Women function in a meeting with women.
3. Men and women function in a meeting together.

This organic birth of freedom takes time, but a day comes when the men and the women both will be themselves, and both will be comfortable. The secret is simple. First become comfortable with your gender.

While I was writing this chapter I witnessed a living, breathing example of what I was writing about.

The church has a special Lord's banquet* every spring. The time came for the church to begin planning for the banquet. Anticipating the possible difficulties in making timely decisions, someone (a woman) was selected to keep order in the planning meeting, if possible. (She would have been more accurately called a referee!)

The meeting started well enough, but soon there was laughter, teasing, puns, and there would have been an almost total breakdown of purpose (except for the competent referee). Everyone was enjoying being together! Finally the plans were made. The church would rent a big room, have roasted lamb, and in the middle of the banquet, the bread and cup would be brought out and everyone would share. There were toasts, songs, laughter, joy and tears. This is what happens when two freed genders get together.

The next chapter is a partial list of experiences this church had in just one year.

---

*It is a Lord's Supper, but we make it a two- or three-hour celebration.

Twenty-Four

Creativity Turned Loose

Here are experiences that the body of Christ did as brothers and sisters.

Keep in mind, this church had no minister. Ministry is in the hands of the men and women of the church. Also keep in mind that you are reading of unleashed creativity *in the church*. This was not done by a small segment of the members. These were church-wide activities.

1. The men decided to throw a banquet for the women. The men sent out invitations, asking the women to come dressed semi-formal. The men cooked the meal, prepared the table, etc. When the women entered, each woman was given a rose and a handwritten note reminding her who she is in Christ. The meal was scrumptious. Each woman had a waiter. The brotherhood served the women, carrying a towel over their left arm. The women were bowled over. Was this a once-in-a-lifetime experience? No, it was fairly typical of how the men treated the women of the church.

2. A month or so later the women reciprocated. They cooked and served a meal to the men except,

141

as usual, the women were even more creative. (There is a sense of admiration in both the sisterhood and brotherhood.)

3. All the women in the church were invited to have dinner on a river boat. The men drove them to the port in limousines.* The men stood on the wharf and sang the women off on their cruise. When the women arrived back, the men were waiting on the wharf, singing to them again and seeing them home.

4. The women went on a weekend camping trip, while all the men together took care of all the children.

5. The men went on a weekend canoe trip, came back and put on a skit for the entire church, demonstrating what the weekend was like. Each man imitated the adventures and eccentricities of another man. (It was hysterical.)

6. Women often break in on the men's meeting to sing, encourage and admonish. The men do the same. Both come as surprises to the other.

7. The entire direction of the church was turned over to the women. They had all the church responsibility for three months.

(The goal of all ministry, whether by men or women or all, is to present Christ.)

By the way, when men make decisions about church direction, there is one sacred rule: If the women do not approve, they have veto power. (This is not a democracy.)

---

*Unfortunately, the man in charge of providing limousines changed his mind and rented vans. No one has ever let him live it down!

8. From time to time, a meeting will begin with the men singing a number of songs to the women (previously practiced in secret). So also the reverse.

9. The men drew names out of a hat, each taking the name of one of the women. The men prepared a dinner for the women. During the meal each man took the name of the one he drew and spoke words of encouragement to that woman. He told what she means to the church. (Yes, there were a lot of tears.) Be sure, in all this, the men in the church are held in high esteem. So are the women.

10. Every month each single woman in the church is contacted by men to discover if that unmarried woman has any practical needs the men could care for.

11. The women take a day off while all the men care for all the children, freeing the women from responsibility.

12. Women go to other cities to encourage the women—or everyone—in other churches. So do the men.

13. Messages are brought to the entire church by different people. While I was writing this book a sister in Christ astounded the church with a full-length message on the Lord's feast. It was fantastic, and it was as natural as breathing that this would happen. Is she some very special woman in the church? Many did not even know she could speak. This takes place with no great "specialness" about it.

Something special is done a half-dozen times every year. Whatever it is, it is planned weeks in advance.

How does all this affect the men? The men respect and marvel at the women. (The women feel the same way about the men.)

Does all this affect the relationship of husband and wife? To find the answer to that, I asked the women of that church to get together and provide answers which I promised I would place in this book.

Twenty-Five

An Interview
with Christian Women

After I finished this book, all the women in my home church met to talk with me.

I asked acid-test questions.

"You know the contents of this book. I have stated that you have lived the reality of this book and that you are truly free women. Is it true? Do you live in freedom? Do you *know*? Are you certain that you live in freedom? Are there any of you who live in the sense of an overhanging shadow of some invisible conformity? Do you have any sense that men control you? Do you have a sense of something you are supposed to conform to? Are there certain unstated expectations? Are there certain things you do not feel free to talk about?"

Then I ventured a question that was, for me, the most important question: "You are familiar with the passage in Ephesians calling for women's submission (even though the word is in italics). I ask you to reflect on this question. Before you were in the church, it was just you and your husband. Today you are part of a corporate community. In which situation did you feel more comfortable with your husband? In which of these two situations was your relationship with your husband better?"

The response to the question?

(The women sitting in the room began talking to one another! Then consensus was reached.)

"I am much more willing to go along with my husband's leadership *in church life* than I ever was before we came into this experience of the body of Christ."

Then this question followed:

"In this book I state that a woman in church life is safer than anywhere else. Meaning that the church would not tolerate any abuse by a man toward his wife. Either the brothers would not tolerate this and/or the women would not tolerate it. Am I correct in this statement?"

Once more the women spoke to one another and then to me. Here was their answer:

"If a woman in the church is being mistreated by her husband, if she will let someone in the church know—preferably another woman—then the situation will very definitely be dealt with. But, if this mistreatment is unknown to others, if the woman prefers to not let it be known, then, of course, nothing will be done.

So it is, and so it can be.

Twenty-Six

Some Final Words

How can such freedom be yours?

A Final Word to Women

Freedom must first be found inside.

And you need to hear the message of this book again and again. (Therefore, I entreat Christian workers of future generations to stand for the equality of Christian women and to build again a matrix of freedom in each generation.)

As long as we have these tragic mistranslations found in four passages penned by Paul, there will be men who will seek to subjugate you.

Dear sisters in Christ, let no man or woman put you in bondage.

A Message to Christian Workers

I call on ministers across the ages to think outside the box. Better still, get out of that box! It will take men called of God, courageous men, who have absolute and total trust of laymen! Men who will place brotherhood and sisterhood above any sense of direction that comes from invisible expectations for conformity.

I cannot say to you, "Allow women to have their freedom." In Christ that freedom has already been given to women. But I do call on men who are called of God: Create an atmosphere in which that freedom emerges in a practical and living way.

For that to happen will require a new breed of workers.

Right now the Christian world is a dangerous place for women.

In Closing

It is my hope that this book stays in print for scores of years or until a better one is written to take its place.

How free was Jesus Christ in the bosom of the Father, in realms unseen? How free was Jesus Christ in the presence of His Father, in realms visible? How free was Jesus Christ as He lived in the jungle of rules, regulations and the imprisoning powers of religion?

And now Lord, raise up workers who will get out of the box and give the Christian world a new way of knowing Jesus Christ . . . a new way of making Jesus Christ central in all things.

My dear sister in Christ, you are free and you are free indeed. As you lay down this book, I ask of you that, henceforth and forevermore, you be at the very least . . . *free inside*.

—Gene Edwards

First at the Cradle, Last at the Cross

Dorothy Sayers put it very well when she wrote:

Perhaps it is no wonder that the women were first at the Cradle and last at the Cross. They had never known a man like this Man—there never has been such another. A prophet and teacher who never nagged at them, never flattered or coaxed or patronized; who never made arch jokes about them, never treated them as "The women, God help us!"or "The ladies, God bless them!"; who rebuked without querulousness and praised without condescension; who took their questions and arguments seriously; who never mapped out their sphere for them, never urged them to be feminine or jeered at them for being female; who had no axe to grind and no uneasy male dignity to defend; who took them as he found them and was completely unselfconscious. There is no act, no sermon, no parable in the whole Gospel that borrows its pungency from female perversity; nobody could possibly guess from the words and deeds of Jesus that there was anything "funny" about woman's nature.*

------

*Loren Cunningham and David Joel Hamilton, *Why Not Women?* (Seattle: YWAM Publishing, ©2000), pg.112. Used with permission.*

On the following pages are the signatures of women who are testifying to the fact that they are both free and equal in the daily living and the direction of their experience in church life.

Signatures

155

Heide Ferguson

Brenda Underwood

Lisa R. Nelson

Elizabeth Massey

Carol Lewis

Nicole Schmid

Ruth Eisses

Alisa Booth

Judi Nelson

Susan L. Justice

Melissa A. Thomas

Cindy Stallings

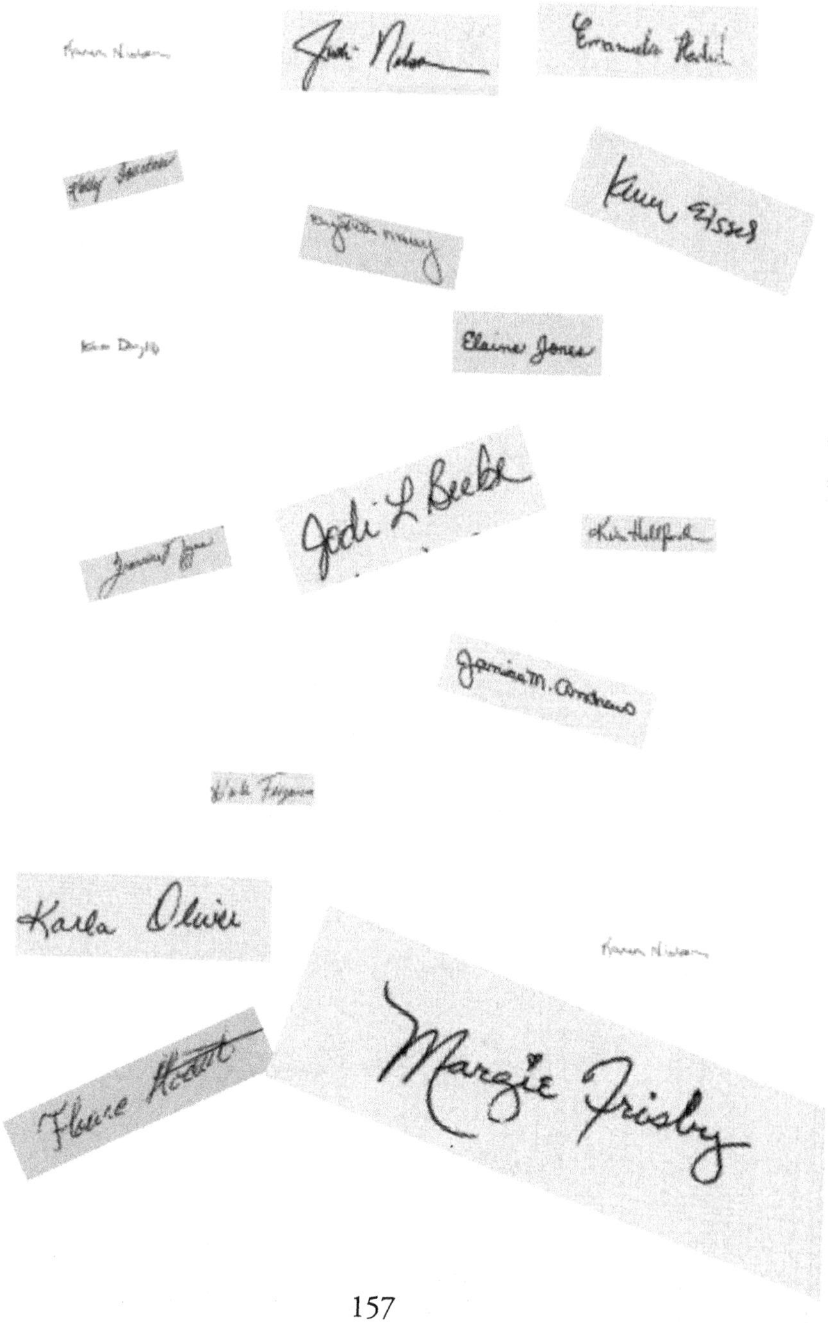
Elaine Jones
Jodi L Beebe
Margie Frisby

Mary Santo

Judi Keener

Anita DeGiz

April Carter

Amanda Sanford

Connie Davis

Tricia E. Sanford-Speiser

Elaine Jones

Jamice M. Andrews

Diane McKennedy

Patricia E. Sanford

ADDENDA

WOMEN WORKERS

"Should a woman be a Christian worker?"

The answer is simple. Absolutely, *if* she can survive the training! But that is the part that is overlooked. The question is not whether or not a woman can be a worker. Here is the same question: "Can men be workers?" Yes, if they can survive the training. In both questions it is a matter of survival.

It has fallen my lot to train Christian workers. Again, step out of the box with me. In the world I live in, *any* man (or woman) who professes to be called of God must first become an ordinary brother (or an ordinary sister) in the church. There . . . you will be known. The church will come to know *you*! You will first live as a layperson and not "in the cloth." There has been many a man who has tried and failed at being a *brother*. Instead he keeps on being a minister, or he flunks Brotherhood 101. He wants to pontificate in the brothers' meeting . . . and all the meetings, when he shares. He prays with a deep baritone voice that rolls beautifully. He speaks in King James English. (Actually, there are a thousand ways for a man "called" to flunk brotherhood. So also a woman to flunk sisterhood.)

Many do not even bother to enroll in Church Life 101 when they find out they have to *also* get a job and work for a living.

Do you really think this free-swinging church is going to choose a professional to be *their* worker? Those Christians have outgrown pontification . . . and other religious trappings . . . as well as any kind of one-up-manship or overlording.

No, the brothers in the ekklesia will not abide such a man. The same is true for a woman.

A woman professes to be called of God? No one will dispute that, but when she steps into a sisters' meeting and begins to be special, or anything leaks out that tells of professionalism, or being more insightful than others, then she is very definitely going to flunk receiving the approval of the church. Actually, it really is not quite like that. Church life will change you into a normal human or you will not survive.

That is the church's part, causing you to be normal.

Next comes the training part.

What is it like to be in a room with a group of men and women being trained (not in a seminary classroom nor in a Bible school) by an old man who has planted churches? He will talk to those young men and women about being servants, about not being leaders, about dying to their own nature, about never correcting God's people, about living highly disciplined lives, about never being pushy or spiteful . . . about being patient beyond words.

It is unbelievable how many men cannot lay down control, cannot lay down a correcting spirit, cannot lay down their temperament, cannot lay down petty feelings, cannot survive in the presence of corporate leadership. Some lose their Elizabethan English but keep their hot temper. They get their feelings hurt.

They play games with other people's heads. One of the most difficult things men in training have found is simply to say "I was wrong." (You would think saying "I was wrong" automatically breaks the jaw.)

Guess who flunks such people?

It is not the one doing the training! It is the church.

The standard is *the same* for both men and women. So, you have your answer.

The obstacle course is on level ground.

What is expected of one is expected of all.

The most difficult thing to do for anyone who feels he is called of God is to stop acting like he is!

You will have to be a brother in church life before you become a worker in church life! You are going to have to be a sister in church life before you will be a worker in the church. Ah, but it gets tougher. Can such men and women also reach the following standards?

"Can you work for a living?"

"Sir, can you earn your own wages?

Can you get a job just like the rest of us regular people? Can you spend most if not all of the rest of your life working for a living and not depending on your income being derived from your ministry?" (When you get to the point you are dependent on God's people for your livelihood, you have lost the prophetic edge.)

Dear sister in Christ, do you feel called of God? Brother do you? Then, are you prepared to be prepared first-century style?

If so, then look us up.

Here is the unconscious thought that will decide your fate: The Lord's people will be saying to themselves, "Do I want this person to be my worker?"

This is how all men—and women—should be trained.

This kind of training is the kind of training that will produce the desperately needed new breed of workers!

May God hasten the day when the church of Jesus Christ will be able to stand up and say, "These women are precious in God's sight. They know Him. They have been ordinary in the presence of the sisterhood and the brotherhood. They are neither pretentious nor religious. They love Him. They experience Him. And they bear His image. All signs point that they are called—and they are not a danger to God's people."

God is looking for such believers, be they men or women.

The Embarrassed Husband

You have heard the following statement: It is a shame for a woman to speak in the . . . (The missing word is not what you think.)

The word that goes in the blank is *ekklesia*. But what is the meaning of the word *ekklesia*? The answer is, the word *ekklesia* does not mean *church*. And *ekklesia* should never be translated *church*. It should be translated *assembly*. (Why *ekklesia* is always translated *church* goes back to Jerome.)

Let us look at the sentence again.

"It is a shame for a woman to speak in the assembly."

Now you have two possible interpretations of that passage: the secular assembly or the Christian assembly.

Is there a way to know which interpretation is correct? Yes. And it is not a reference to the Christian assembly (the church) but a secular assembly (a secular assembly called by the government of a city).

In I Corinthians Fourteen there is a key word that tells us this. That word is *law*.

For sure the word *law* does not refer to the law of Moses. Then what law is being referred to here?

Paul was answering some kind of question. But what was the question?

Here is a possible example:

"My wife goes with me to the assembly of the city fathers. She speaks out. She asks a question and gives her opinions. I am embarrassed. She says, 'I can speak in the assembly of God's people, why can I not speak in the governmental assembly?'"

Look at that strange statement, "they are to subject themselves just as the law says." Paul's use of *law* simply cannot be a reference to the Jewish law.

First, there is no place in the Old Testament that says a woman is not permitted to speak in a meeting.

Secondly, Paul is the author of the blistering letter to the Galatians. His Galatian letter was written before he wrote Corinthians. In Galatians, would Paul, writing to a Gentile/Greek church, ask them to obey the Mosaic law, when he himself had stated in Galatians that the Mosaic law had been nailed to the cross? The law of Moses was taken into the grave, and it has been nullified.

But there was a law! It was a local, secular law. In Corinth there was a law that a woman could not speak in the secular ekklesia (assembly). Women are forbidden to speak when the city magistrates are presiding over the local "town hall meeting."

We do not know exactly what question Paul responded to. Did Paul say women in the local Christian assembly should stop disrupting the meetings with chit-chat and questions?

But the problem with the word law persists. Maybe, just maybe, the question came from a Roman woman who was accustomed to speaking out on anything, anytime she wanted.

Was Paul saying to her, "Women are to keep silent in the secular assemblies, for they are not permitted by law to speak"?

Women were supposed to listen while at the secular assembly and then ask questions when they got home. This fits the Greek view of women perfectly.

Remember, in Corinth, women were not supposed to go to the marketplace. They were not supposed to speak to men. Neither were they to say anything in the governmental assembly. City leaders called meetings, came and sat down on a platform called a bema. Men came and they talked, but women had no input.

It can be stated with all certainty: It would be wonderful if all future translators of the New Testament would translate that word *ekklesia* as *assembly* rather than to use the word *church*. It would save a great deal of pain for women. This translation would help all of us to realize that an assembly is not necessarily a religious service. The word *ekklesia* can be used to describe any gathering of people.

Here is the bottom line. Anyone who embraces the silence of women in a Christian gathering is doing so in the face of everything else in Paul's ministry, as well as the rest of the New Testament. It is only fair to translate this passage correctly . . . *assembly*. The word *church* is an out-and-out mistranslation.

Once more, we have a new view of this passage. At the minimum, we have the choice of two views. Which you choose says volumes about your understanding of a woman's position in Christ and in the church.

SeedSowers
800-228-2665 (fax) 866-252-5504
www.seedsowers.com

Revolutionary Books on Church Life

Beyond Radical *(Edwards)* 7.95
How to Meet In Homes *(Edwards)* 10.95
An Open Letter to House Church Leaders *(Edwards)* 5.00
When the Church Was Led Only by Laymen *(Edwards)* 5.00
Revolution, The Story of the Early Church *(Edwards)* 11.95
The Silas Diary *(Edwards)* 9.99
The Titus Diary *(Edwards)* 8.99
The Timothy Diary *(Edwards)* 9.99
The Priscilla Diary *(Edwards)* 9.99
The Gaius Diary *(Edwards)* 10.99
Overlooked Christianity *(Edwards)* 10.95
Pagan Christianity *(Viola)* 13.95

An Introduction to the Deeper Christian Life

Living by the Highest Life *(Edwards)* 10.99
The Secret to the Christian Life *(Edwards)* 9.99
The Inward Journey *(Edwards)* 10.99

Classics on the Deeper Christian Life

Experiencing the Depths of Jesus Christ *(Guyon)* 9.95
Practicing His Presence *(Lawrence/Laubach)* 9.95
The Spiritual Guide *(Molinos)* 8.95
Union With God *(Guyon)* 8.95
The Seeking Heart *(Fenelon)* 9.95
Intimacy with Christ *(Guyon)* 10.95
Spiritual Torrents *(Guyon)* 10.95
The Ultimate Intention *(Fromke)* 10.00
One Hundred Days in the Secret Place *(Edwards)* 12.99

In a Class by Itself

The Divine Romance *(Edwards)* 11.99

New Testament

The Story of My Life as Told by Jesus Christ *(Four gospels blended)* 14.95
The Day I was Crucified as Told by Jesus the Christ 14.99
Acts in First Person *(Book of Acts)* 9.95

Commentaries by Jeanne Guyon

Genesis Commentary 10.95
Exodus Commentary 10.95
Leviticus - Numbers - Deuteronomy Commentaries 12.95
Judges Commentary 7.95
Job Commentary 10.95
Song of Songs *(Song of Solomon Commentary)* 9.95
Jeremiah Commentary 7.95
James - I John - Revelation Commentaries 12.95

(Prices subject to change)

THE CHRONICLES OF HEAVEN *(Edwards)*

Christ Before Creation 8.99
The Beginning 8.99
The Escape 8.99
The Birth 8.99
The Triumph 8.99
The Return 8.99

THE COLLECTED WORKS OF T. AUSTIN-SPARKS

The Centrality of Jesus Christ 19.95
The House of God 29.95
Ministry 29.95
Service 19.95
Spiritual Foundations 29.95
The Things of the Spirit 10.95
Prayer 14.95
The On-High Calling 10.95
Rivers of Living Water 8.95
The Power of His Resurrection 8.95

COMFORT AND HEALING

A Tale of Three Kings *(Edwards)* 8.99
The Prisoner in the Third Cell *(Edwards)* 7.99
Letters to a Devastated Christian *(Edwards)* 7.95
Exquisite Agony *(Edwards)* 9.95
Dear Lillian *(Edwards)* *paperback* 5.95
Dear Lillian *(Edwards)* *hardcover* 9.99

OTHER BOOKS ON CHURCH LIFE

Climb the Highest Mountain *(Edwards)* 12.95
The Torch of the Testimony *(Kennedy)* 14.95
The Passing of the Torch *(Chen)* 9.95
Going to Church in the First Century *(Banks)* 5.95
When the Church was Young *(Loosley)* 8.95
Church Unity *(Litzman,Nee,Edwards)* 10.95
Let's Return to Christian Unity *(Kurosaki)* 10.95
Rethinking the Wineskin *(Viola)* 9.95
Who Is Your Covering? *(Viola)* 8.95

CHRISTIAN LIVING

Your Lord Is a Blue Collar Worker *(Edwards)* 7.95
The Autobiography of Jeanne Guyon 19.95
Final Steps in Christian Maturity *(Guyon)* 12.95
Turkeys and Eagles *(Lord)* 9.95
The Life of Jeanne Guyon *(T.C. Upham)* 17.95
Life's Ultimate Privilege *(Fromke)* 10.00
Unto Full Stature *(Fromke)* 10.00
All and Only *(Kilpatrick)* 8.95
Adoration *(Kilpatrick)* 9.95
Release of the Spirit *(Nee)* 9.99
Bone of His Bone *(Huegel)* *modernized* 8.95
You can Witness with Confidence *(Rinker)* 10.95

The Divine Romance
by
Gene Edwards

The Divine Romance is praised as one of the all-time literary achievements of the Protestant era. Breathtakingly beautiful, here is the odyssey of Christ's quest for His bride. *The Divine Romance* is the most captivating, heartwarming and inspirational romance, transcending space and time. In all of Christian literature there has never been a description of the crucifixion and resurrection which so rivals the one depicted in *The Divine Romance*.

Many readers have commented, "This book should come with a box of Kleenex." The description of the romance between Adam and Eve alone is one of the great love stories of all times.

Edwards' portrayal of the romance of Christ and his bride takes its place along side such classics as Dante's *The Divine Comedy* and Milton's *Paradise Lost*. Reading this literary masterpiece will alter your life forever.

One of the greatest Christian classics of all time.

An Introduction to
The Deeper Christian Life

In Three Volumes

by

Gene Edwards

Living by
the Highest Life

If you find yourself unsettled with Christianity as usual . . . if you find yourself longing for a deeper experience of the Christian life . . . *The Highest Life* is for you.

Did Jesus Christ live the Christian life merely by human effort? Or did Jesus understand living by the Spirit—his Father's Life in him?

Discover what it means to live a spiritual life while living on earth.

I.

The Secret to
the Christian Life

Read the Bible, pray, go to church, tithe . . . is this what it means to live the Christian life? Is there more to living the Christian life than following a set of rules? How did Jesus live by the Spirit?

The Secret to the Christian Life reveals the one central secret to living out the Christian life. Nor does the book stop there . . . it also gives *practical* ways to enhance your fellowship with the Lord.

II.

The Inward Journey

The Inward Journey is the companion volume to *The Secret to the Christian Life*. A beautiful story of a dying uncle explaining to his nephew, a new Christian, the ways and mysteries of the cross and of suffering. Of those who have a favorite Gene Edwards book, tens of thousands have selected *The Inward Journey* as that book.

III.

The First-Century Diaries
by
Gene Edwards

IF YOU NEVER READ ANY OTHER BOOKS ON THE NEW
TESTAMENT . . . READ *THE FIRST-CENTURY DIARIES*!

Here is more than what you would learn
in seminary! The Diaries will revolutionize your
understanding of the New Testament, and, in turn will revolutionize your life. The best part is, this set of diaries reads like a novel.
Never has learning the New Testament been so much fun.

I.

The Silas Diary

This historical narrative parallels the book of Acts, giving a first-person account of Paul's first journey.

The Silas Diary is your invitation to join Silas, Paul, and
their companions on a journey fraught with danger and adventure - a journey that changed the history of the world.
Learn with the first-century Christians what freedom in Christ
really means.

II.

The Titus Diary

This compelling narrative continues the events of the
Book of Acts. *The Titus Diary* is a firsthand account of Paul's
second journey as told by Titus.

Join this journey as Paul sets out once more-this time
with Silas, Timothy, and Luke-and learn of the founding of
the churches in Philippi, Thessalonica, Corinth, and Ephesus.
Look on as Paul meets Aquila and Priscilla and quickly gains
an appreciation of their passion for the Lord and his church.

The First-Century Diaries

III.

The Timothy Diary

In *The Timothy Diary* Paul's young Christian companion Timothy gives a firsthand account of Paul's third journey.

This journey is quite different from Paul's others. It is the fulfillment of Paul's dream, for in Ephesus Paul trains a handful of young men to take his place after his death. Paul follows Christ's example in choosing and training disciples to spread the gospel and encourage the growth of the church.

IV.

The Priscilla Diary

Here are the stories of Paul's continued travels to the first-century churches narrated from the unique perspective of Priscilla, a vibrant first-century Christian woman!

See Paul writing his most personally revealing letter, his letter to the church in Corinth. Marvel at the truths Paul conveys to the church in Rome, a letter "of all that Paul considered central to the Christian life."

V.

The Gaius Diary

Paul and Nero meet face to face in a moment of highest drama.

Paul is released, but soon is arrested again, and again faces Nero. The sentence is death. Just before his execution, all the men he trained arrived in Rome to be with him. *The Gaius Diary* gives life-changing insight into Paul's final letters. Colossians, Ephesians, Philemon, and Philippians come alive as you see in living color the background to these letters. Be there in April of 70 A.D. when Jerusalem is destroyed.

For the first time ever in all church history, here is the entire first-century story from beginning to end.

Books that Heal

Hundreds of thousands of Christians all over the world have received healing while reading these books.

Exquisite Agony
(formerly titled *Crucified by Christians*)

Gene Edwards

Here is healing for hurting and disillusioned Christians who have known the pain of betrayal at the hand of another believer.

This book has brought restoration to Christians all over the world who had lost all hope. Edwards takes you to a high place to see your pain and suffering from the viewpoint of the Lord.

Read this book and learn the *privilege of betrayal* and discover who the real author of your crucifixion is!

Letters to a Devastated Christian

Gene Edwards

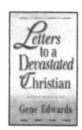

The Christian landscape is covered with the remains of lives ruined at the hands of authoritarian movements. Some believers never recover. Others are the walking wounded.

In *Letters to a Devastated Christian*, Edwards has written a series of letters to a brokenhearted Christian and points him to healing in Christ. This book is full of profound healing and hope.

The Prisoner in the Third Cell

Gene Edwards

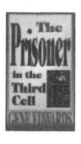

This is a book of comfort, told as an unforgettable drama, for those caught up in circumstances of life they do not understand.

In this dramatic story, John the Baptist, imprisoned by Herod and awaiting death, struggles to understand a Lord who did not live up to his expectations.

If you are a suffering Christian or know of one, this book will bring enormous comfort and insight into the ways of God.

A Tale of Three Kings

Gene Edwards

Myriads of Christians have experienced pain, loss and heartache at the hands of other believers. This compelling story offers comfort, healing and hope for these wounded ones. Probably more Christians have turned to *A Tale of Three Kings* for healing than to any other book for decades.

This simple, powerful, and beautiful story has been recommended by Christians throughout the world.

The Chronicles of Heaven

by

Gene Edwards

In *The Beginning* God creates the heavens and the earth. The crowning glory of creation, man and woman, live and move in both the visible world and the spiritual world.

Experience one of the greatest events of human history: *The Escape* of the Israelite people from Egypt. Watch the drama from the view of earthly participants and the view of angels in the heavens.

Experience the wonderful story of the incarnation, the Christmas story, seen from both realms. *The Birth* introduces the mystery of the Christian life for those who have never heard the story.

In *The Triumph* you will experience the Easter story as you never have before. Join angels as they comprehend the suffering and death of Jesus and the mystery of free will in light of God's Eternal Purpose.

The Door has moved to a hill on Patmos. What would John be allowed to see? *The Return* invites you to witness the finale of the stirring conclusion to *The Chronicles of Heaven*.

CPSIA information can be obtained at www.ICGtesting.com
Printed in the USA
LVOW01s0352290415

436454LV00003B/3/P